# The Road Home

## A Letter
## To My Children

Mimi Morton Buckley

Illustrated by
Aya Morton

RABBIT RABBIT PRESS
Mill Valley, California

*For Mom,*
*you taught me the meaning of home.*

*And for Coleman, Woods, and Lake,*
*who have filled this life with light.*

"It's a long and rugged road
and we don't know where it's headed,
but we know it's gonna get us where we're going.
And when we find what we're looking for,
we'll drop these bags and search no more.
'Cause it's gonna feel like heaven when we're home."
– THE WAILIN' JENNYS


"There are two mistakes one can make along the road
to truth ... not going all the way, and not starting."
– THE BUDDHA

# Contents

# The Invitation

My Dearest Coleman, Woods, and Lake,

Just Add Water. This has been our family motto since the beginning. While we always said it with a laugh, the majority of your lives have been spent either in, on, or by the water, and it does seem to be an easy recipe for the happiness that comes from feeling connected both to ourselves and to the rhythms of our planet. However, as you have probably guessed, there were other ingredients added along the way besides water, and it is these that I would like to share with you.

Like any good recipe, our family culture was created partially by inherited traditions and then enriched through invention. Your father and I distilled many influences from our two very different families, inspiring visions and revisions of what we imagined our future to be. We also learned by watching those who had begun the journey before us, allowing us to benefit from their experiences. But far and away our greatest teachers have been the three of you. Your arrival led us to places we had never traveled to before, while your perfection and vulnerability as new beings inspired us to create an environment that harmonized with your presence. We took our cues from you, adding this collection of lessons learned and wisdom gained to the broth of everyday life, thus creating the family to which you belong.

So, as you can see, over time we have all been guides for one another. Because of my love for it, my particular specialty is the terrain of the home. Ever since I can remember, I have always enjoyed making a home. It began as a very young child, when I would spend hours arranging and rearranging furniture in my dollhouse, creating imaginary meals in the little kitchen and placing miniature vases of flowers in each room. When I went away for high school, I decorated my room with Indian fabrics and comfy pillows so friends would feel welcome to visit and share a pot of tea. During college, I made all of my various living situations as inviting as possible. It was deeply satisfying, even comforting, to offer a place where everyone could gather.

I understand this love of home to be more than the simple pleasure of making a welcoming place. It is born from the desire we all share to experience profound belonging. Creating a harmonious environment is a practical joy that results in a sanctuary for our spirits: a place of nourishment for both body and soul. Our home supports the various thresholds in our lives, including birth, childhood, marriage, old age, and finally culminating in death. It offers a road home to ourselves, unfolding as a journey of self-discovery. Navigating these successive twists and turns of life in an atmosphere that is both open and secure, we learn to rest in ourselves more deeply. This creates an opportunity for reflection, imbuing our actions with greater awareness, which in turn strengthens our relationships with those around us. Feeling at home within ourselves leads naturally to feeling at home with life and allows us to recognize our own relationship to all of creation. A home where these inner and outer landscapes of beauty are cultivated brings comfort and is a safe haven for introspection and renewal. Knowing this instills purpose into each moment, making even the simplest daily task an opportunity for the experience of connection and loving kindness. Weaving this understanding into our lives and expressing it through our actions is a gift, both visible and invisible, to ourselves and others.

The stories that follow are each in their own way an ingredient of the home in which you grew up. Some of these stories you'll recognize, having lived them, but here you'll experience them through my eyes. There may be others who listen in, so I have added some details for clarification with which I am sure you are already familiar.

It was a privilege to be a full-time mother, and I was extremely fortunate to have the financial stability that allowed for this luxury of choice. Yet, by selecting one path instead of another, there is often an element of compromise and even loss. Householding as a spiritual practice gives meaning and depth to the art of homemaking, whose importance as a foundation for happiness is undervalued and often goes unseen. It would appear that homemaking has become another cultural casualty, one easily added to the endangered species list of our world. I want to share these stories with you so we can all remember how valuable a resource it is.

The feeling of home is quite simply the one underlying experience I know that can include birth, death, dinner, and enlightenment all in one breath. So I invite you to come with me—explore the meaning of home and what makes it so.

PART ONE

# STARTING OUT

# Lucky Break

There is a lot of truth in this old saying, for heartbreak, with all of its sadness, also brings with it a deeper appreciation for joy as well as greater empathy for the suffering of others. As we break open our hearts, we can begin to love more fully. However, I was now thirty-two and had already experienced a good amount of this kind of luck in my romantic life. I was ready for something else. The only problem was, I didn't really know what that something else would be. Perhaps the iconic marriage and family wasn't in the cards for me. I was becoming quite comfortable with that idea and could see myself as a successful single woman, defined by my work and a life I loved.

But let me back up several months to a summer afternoon in Los Angeles. I was living on my own and working as an art director for Esprit, an international apparel company. That day, a handsome blond man visiting from the European sister company walked through our office. I greeted him, explaining that my background was in architecture and that I was designing the visual presentation for the new stores. Then I asked him about himself. "Oh, I always wanted to be an architect, but I build things in Germany," he said. Esprit was tremendously generous to its employees, and I assumed he was a carpenter sent from Germany so he could experience firsthand the high level of

7

craftsmanship and design evident in all of the firm's building projects. That was the extent of our contact, and I never even caught his name.

Before taking the position with Esprit, I had lived in Paris for two years and worked with a French architectural firm. It was right around this time of the chance meeting with the carpenter that I had begun to dream about living abroad again. After all, I was single, and in the absence of any real commitments that would tie me down, why not take advantage of my freedom? So that fall (1985) I asked Esprit about available design opportunities in Europe, and within weeks I found myself heading to Germany to help with the opening of their new stores and showrooms. My employer there would be an American named Peter Buckley, an owner of Esprit Europe.

Driving through the chilling blanket of drizzle from the Düsseldorf airport with a gruff taxi driver, I couldn't help but wonder why I had decided to take the job. It had felt like the right time for me to travel and see the world, but living in the equivalent of a gray sock where I didn't speak the language did not feel very tempting. I had heard it said that the people in Düsseldorf called their city "Paris am Rhine," but I was quite certain that I had never heard any French person refer to Paris as *"Düsseldorf sur Seine."* The similarities were not immediately apparent to me, either.

The taxi finally arrived at the Esprit office, and once inside the cheerful, light-filled space, everything began to feel better. The young woman who met me at the door explained that she was Peter's assistant and that he would be free shortly. Because the office was divided by glass walls, I asked if she could point him out to me. "Oh, certainly. That's him right there," she said, gesturing to a tall man who was standing at his desk. There stood the carpenter. I suppressed a laugh, remembering our meeting six months earlier and his self-effacing description of what he did. I immediately liked him.

After a few minutes I was shown into his office, and we discussed the practical arrangements for my time in Düsseldorf. The plan had been for me to stay in the company's guesthouse, but due to a huge fashion convention going on, it was already booked. In addition, all the hotels in the city were packed. Peter handed me the keys to his apartment, explaining that I could use his guest room until other accommodations became available. That was how I found myself at the door of *einundzwanzig* (twenty-one) Rathausufer, a classic Düsseldorf apartment building that Peter had chosen as his home.

A Californian by birth, Peter and his four siblings were born into a military family that moved every eighteen months, depending on where his father, the Commander, was stationed. Peter became a competitive springboard diver as a teenager and received a full athletic scholarship to the University of Washington. After college, he attended Hastings School of Law and later began his own practice in San Francisco. Two years had passed when his friend, Doug Tompkins, the co-owner of Esprit, USA, asked Peter if he would organize trading companies in South America and India. Upon his return from New Delhi, Peter stopped in Düsseldorf to see Doug, who was struggling with a failing Esprit Germany. The company was in the red, and Doug wanted to return to California. In one of those life-changing moments, Peter put his hand into his pocket and pulled out one German Mark which he offered to Doug in exchange for the nearly bankrupt business. Doug accepted the offer.

Taking on the responsibility of being the new CEO, Peter learned German on the fly as well as the ins and outs of the clothing business. He familiarized himself with everything from buttons to spreadsheets, gaining the respect of all the employees with whom he worked shoulder to shoulder. By the time I met him, he had lived in Düsseldorf for over ten years and had created one of the most successful fashion companies in Europe.

The name Peter is derived from the Greek word Petros, meaning rock. In fact, Peter's name suited him perfectly. His solid presence carried with it an unwavering quality of integrity. At the age of forty he remained unmarried, fuel for countless articles about the eligible Kalifornier bachelor in all of the popular German magazines. But for me, none of this mattered. The few things I knew for certain at that time included don't lose your passport, floss daily, and never jeopardize a career you love for a flirtation with romance. I loved my job, and Peter was off limits.

We spent the next two weeks working side by side, preparing for the grand opening of Esprit's new showroom and office, a building designed by Milano-based Ettore Sottsass and his design team known as Memphis. With a guest list of over two thousand, the party was the highlight of the week's events, while the building was considered groundbreaking in the world of international architecture. Our time together, though completely enjoyable, remained well within the bounds of a professional relationship. Even so, throughout the focused and creative period of preparation, I felt myself falling for this man. He was smart, funny, and complicated. There was always something interesting going on around him that more often than not he had thought up and instigated. I couldn't deny that he had caught my attention.

His home mirrored the feeling of his presence: sophistication paired with a casual attitude that hadn't missed the sixties. This unassuming man in his denim work shirt and tennis shoes possessed refined sensibilities and a love of fine art. The Düsseldorf apartment was both informal and elegant, where paintings from Bacon, Haring, and Botero mingled with family photos and brightly colored quilts. An air of intelligent simplicity filled the rooms, making it an easy place to relax. Our conversations linked us, revealing a mutual love for Eastern philosophy, the ocean, India, bread baking, and the color yellow.

At the end of the second week of my stay, a group of friends gathered with us at his apartment for drinks before heading off to see a performance of Chinese acrobats. One of the guests, an attractive German woman, walked directly into his bedroom and threw her coat on the bed with an intimate familiarity—a clear gesture of staking her territory. That's when I felt it: a jolt of jealousy. My inner adult jumped to the rescue, thoroughly alarmed and demanding that I resist the feeling for fear it could spell nothing but trouble. Besides, I had just wrapped up another attempt at romance with a French boyfriend. The roadmap of his soul promised too many dead-ends and detours, and it wasn't a journey I wanted to take.

It was as clear as the coat on the bed. Now was the time to set my emotional compass on friendship. That would have to be enough, I kept telling myself, or at least I tried to. Somewhere during the course of the evening, between the Chinese acrobats' first cartwheels and their last handstands, the needle on my compass began to spin. The magnetic attraction between our two poles was unstoppable. A new course was being charted.

Driving along the gray Autobahn the next morning, Peter asked, "How's your French boyfriend?" I told him there wasn't one and asked him back, "How's your German girlfriend?" He laughed and said he didn't think he was going to have one much longer. Those few words were all that were said on the subject. It was a short yet clarifying conversation that held a sense of possibility at its edges. But there was no time to ponder it as the opening was just days away, and there were notebooks full of details to complete—finalizing the layout of the event, last minute adjustments of the lighting and sound, styling the clothing and accessories, arranging the flowers and food. Romance was not on the list.

The event was an absolute success, and all of our hard work had paid off. Late in the evening as the huge gala party was winding down, I found myself sitting in a quiet corner looking out over the dance floor. I was both relieved and pleased that it had all gone so well. Quite unexpectedly, a warm river of shivers flowed down my back—an electrical current ending in my toes. Only in the next moment did I realize that Peter was behind me, having gently kissed the nape of my neck.

"Are you ready to go home?" he asked.

All I could say was, "Definitely."

Three months later, just before dozing off for the night, he turned to me as he leaned on one elbow and said, "You are going to marry me, aren't you?" I loved how simply he asked such a huge, life-defining question. It reflected the ease we felt with one another and predicted the way we would make our choices ever since. "Of course," I responded, and we dropped off to sleep in each other's arms.

# Take the Plunge

*"You take two bodies and you twirl them into one;*
*their hearts and their bones and they won't come undone."*

– PAUL SIMON

M y experience with the prospect of marriage, though not extensive, was colorful. I had been stood up at the altar three years
prior and was still rattled by the idea of a large wedding. This
heart-shattering incident occurred two days before our planned union,
when the man I thought was my true love looked me squarely in the
eyes and informed me that he was not going to be available, then or
ever. Knowing this history, I am sure you can understand why I was re-
luctant to send out invitations again; I had returned enough wedding
presents for a lifetime.

Fortunately, Peter and I were of one mind when it came to imagining how we would be married, and we decided that a small gathering
would suit our needs. In late summer of 1986, we organized a sailing
trip to the Grenadines, a chain of remote islands in the Caribbean, and
invited four friends to join us. We didn't tell them our plans, preferring
the decision to remain simply between the two of us. With no one in-
fluencing the day, time, or place of the wedding, we had absolute confidence that we would know when the time was right.

Late one afternoon, our boat came to rest among a small grouping
of three palm-fringed islands whose sand was pink from conch shells.

The disappearing sun painted the sky as we plunged into a sea so alive with phosphorescence that our every movement released a multitude of stars. A balmy evening, complete with good friends and a delicious dinner, left both of us thoroughly satisfied. Falling asleep opposite one another, we were just close enough to reach across the cockpit and hold hands. The limitless night sky glowed above us. All in the same moment my inner army of guards decided the battle was over. My heart, broken open, knew it was safe to come out. All uncertainty sparked and vanished, like the phosphorescence, into the dark sea.

I woke to the rhythmic lapping against the hull. Surrounded by sunrise and the quiet coolness of morning, I turned to find Peter. He was already awake, and his gaze anchored me. I felt safe to proceed. Somehow we both knew that this was the day.

We told everyone aboard of the plan. Although surprised, they adjusted to the news with enthusiasm and went about decorating the boat with palm fronds and nautical flags. Perched on the cabin bunks below, Peter and I wrote our vows while warm raindrops and a double rainbow punctuated the morning sky. Daniel, our skipper, appalled that I had not come prepared with a wedding dress, appeared with a bolt of mosquito netting that had been stored in the hull of the ship. Katie and Gilda, assuming the role of bridesmaids, began cutting and draping the white cloud of fabric, and by noon I was wrapped in an impromptu wedding dress (with a veil ten feet long!).

A gentle breeze returned the sky to a bright blue as we gathered barefoot on the wooden deck and formed a semicircle at the stern of the boat. The musky smell of wet teak and salt blended with wafts of caramel-cream wedding cake baking in the galley. Sea birds called out from overhead while colorful flags furled and snapped, framing the bright white sail against the blue.

The ceremony was slightly confusing. Our German friend Hans Martin, a theological school graduate, began to translate into English the lines he could remember from a traditional German wedding to Daniel, who, as the boat's captain, had the power to marry us on board ship. The problem with this approach was that Daniel, who has a very thick French accent, couldn't understand Hans Martin's English and so filled in the ceremony with what sounded right to him at the time. Perhaps it would have gone more smoothly if we hadn't all enjoyed that delicious French champagne while we were waiting for the skies to clear. In any case, the entire party was doubled over laughing before we had even gotten close to the "I do" part.

When imagining a sailboat wedding, I had always thought that the best part of the experience would be diving into the sea once the ceremony was over. Sometime after Peter spoke his vows, I lost track of where we were. Everything felt so complete that I thought my dream moment had arrived, so I enthusiastically leapt overboard. It wasn't until I surfaced and saw everyone looking at me from the deck that I realized I had jumped the gun. My unspoken vows, along with bits of wedding dress, floated several feet away. Peter's look of confusion turned to laughter, and he plunged in to join me. The vows could wait; our life had begun.

# The Voice

*"I know the voices in my head aren't real,*
*but sometimes they have really good ideas."*
– MARK ZUCKERBERG

The day of our wedding was an ideal start to our hoped-for lifetime of adventure. In fact, the adventure began right away. The following afternoon on board was a relaxed one, with everyone melting into various pastimes such as reading, naps, and daydreams. The pink sand was calling to me, so I strapped on my mask and fins for a short swim to the island. Floating in the warmth of the clear water, I could see scores of conch resting on the sandy bottom, visited by occasional schools of curious fish. Soon I was in shallow waters, and I clambered out with no particular plan in mind except to find a shady spot under a palm.

Since the wedding, I had enjoyed a particular buoyancy of spirit. It was a feeling that I had not experienced since my childhood. Being loved by Peter so completely replenished my soul, like taking a deep breath for the first time in years. It was a returning to myself, bringing with it a new appreciation for life and a sense of excitement about what lay ahead. I settled into the warm sand, relishing this new state of being. After what must have been about ten minutes of resting quietly, I was suddenly addressed by a deeply resonant male voice which carried with it a tone of absolute certainty. "You are pregnant with a boy. He will be creative and intelligent."

Startled, I sat up and looked around to see where the voice was coming from. I wasn't completely surprised to discover I was alone. The voice had come from within, and I could still feel its presence. A wash of elation flowed through me. I knew the words were true, even while my common sense was shaking its head. Peter and I had imagined our life with children, and this would be a most welcome baby. Still, hearing a voice relaying life-changing news was both shocking and unbelievable. Did I tell my new husband that his wife was hearing voices? Well, I was, so why not? I swam back to the boat and told Peter the story. It did seem a little far-fetched. Deciding that there was nothing to do or not do, we both said "Wow!" and promptly forgot about it.

A month later, we were on an airplane headed for Costa Rica to join a rafting trip on the Pacuare River. During the previous week I had been feeling queasy on and off, so I asked Peter if he thought it might be the flu. I explained my symptoms, noting that it was especially difficult in the mornings, but that I always felt better after a little breakfast. As soon as the words were spoken we both came to the same realization: pregnant! If it hadn't been for the glowing red seat belt sign, we would have jumped up and down with delight. The voice was right. We both laughed at the mystery of it all, ecstatic to begin the adventure of parenthood. To this day, that is the only time I have ever heard such a voice, and I still wonder—Who was that guy?

# Spiel mit deinem Kind

*"Birthing is so integral with life—so common—that choices
surrounding it often get relegated to chance. We tend to
go along with what everyone else is doing, assuming that
must be for the best. Living in a technological society,
we tend to think that the best of everything is the most
expensive kind available. This is generally true, whether we
are talking about cell phones, cameras, cars or computers.
When it comes to birth, it ain't necessarily so."*

– INA MAY GASKIN

We don't have to do this." Peter looked at me across the olive-green waiting room filled with three mismatched chairs and a couch that looked like the cat had gotten to it. I was seven months pregnant, and we were still searching for a doctor. We had also been married for seven months and were living in Düsseldorf. The only thing that sounded worse to me than having a hospital birth was having a hospital birth in a foreign country. From my perspective, hospitals took away one's personal control, and I definitely wanted to be in control of this experience. I dreamed of a birth without trauma: no medication, no bright lights, no loud voices, no strangers. Considering it from the baby's perspective, it just seemed like learning how to breathe and being right-side up for the first time would be difficult enough without the shock of being washed and weighed. I definitely wanted to be at home.

At first we thought that because we were living in Europe, such a notion would be fully supported and possible. Wasn't this the land of midwives and home births? Wasn't America the place where medicated hospital births were the norm, and women were scheduling appointments to deliver their babies at a convenient moment for the doctor? I was inspired to have our baby at home by Ina May Gaskin, the most famous midwife in the United States. She learned about birth through the process of delivering her own babies. She then trained others in the field of midwifery and has since delivered over 2,000 infants. Armed with her book, *Spiritual Midwifery,* we began to search for a German doctor who would support our plans for a natural birth at home.

As it turned out, we were in the wrong country. If we had been in Holland, finding a midwife would have been relatively easy. But here in Germany things had changed. Those old values were viewed with disdain or at least met with the response, "Why in the world wouldn't you want to be in the hospital? Do you want to risk your baby's life?" So by month seven we were ready to deliver our own baby, just like Ina May. Even if we didn't have help, at least we would be in familiar surroundings. This idea wasn't one that I was exactly wild to share with the folks back home in California. Even I didn't really want to picture in too much detail the scene of two know-nothings trying to deliver their own baby.

One evening while having dinner with neighbors, we hesitantly (for the hundredth time) explained our strategy for birthing our baby, with or without a doctor. One of the other guests told us of a local obstetrician, Dr. Djalali, who performed occasional home births, but only if he felt the couple were right for the experience. That is how we found ourselves staring at each other across a table of German vocational magazines in the unlit waiting room, wondering if we should make a break for it. Before we could tiptoe past the cheerful receptionist, the doctor called out our name: "Bookley?" The door to his office was partially open, serving as a light source for the dismal waiting room. Once again the voice called out "Bookley?" Peter and I, with a "What have we got to lose?" look at one another, proceeded toward the beckoning call.

It was as though we had entered another world. Sunlight poured in through the high windows of the spacious office, creating a halo effect around Dr. Djalali, who sat behind a gleaming, wooden desk. Dressed all in white with a shaven head and an open, intelligent face, he rose to meet us. His smile felt like yet another light had been turned on in the room. As he stood, I saw a very fit Persian man in his early forties whose presence enveloped us both with a feeling of kindness and deep calm. I was amazed at how radiant he appeared, as though illuminated from some inner brightness.

He gestured for us to make ourselves comfortable in the two chairs that faced him. We took our seats, and I began to feel a glimmer of possibility. Although he was speaking German, I felt at ease in his presence. My grasp of the language was childlike at best, the result of a ten-day intensive language immersion class which had given me the ability to successfully navigate the local open-air market. I could comfortably ask for two kilos of potatoes while greeting the friendly produce man, but not much more. Even so, I was getting the basic drift. He liked us. We liked him. The image of Peter preparing to deliver our baby with a bowl of hot water and a pair of scissors simply disappeared. We had found our doctor.

The appointment concluded with me on my back, stethoscope pressed lightly on my belly, while we all listened to the baby's heartbeat for the first time. Our new doctor explained that there would be as little intervention as possible between that time and the birth. He told us that since this is the one opportunity to perceive a soul as pure being rather than identify it through gender, it is best to honor that perception. He encouraged us to enjoy this time of not knowing and to wait until the moment of birth to discover if we had a girl or a boy. We then asked what sort of special things we should be doing to get ready for the birth. He just said, "Be happy, breathe, make love, and oh, play with the baby." Play with the baby? Maybe it was my German. Peter was translating, but even he looked confused.

"*Ja, spiel mit deinem Kind.*" Then he explained. He told me to put my hands on the baby and love it with my heart to the right. Really? I

19

liked this guy, and we needed a doctor, so I gave it my best. I wrapped all the love I felt for this unknown being around it and imagined pulling it gently toward the right. Amazingly, the big lump moved easily under my hands. Then I did the same thing again, only this time to the left. Once again the baby slid effortlessly across to my left side. We all started laughing, and Dr. Djalali instructed me to pull the baby with love toward my heart. *"Zieh' das Kind zum Herz."* Barely believing our eyes, we could see the baby moving up close to my heart. *"Ja!"* He smiled. *"Spiel mit deinem Kind."*

# Coleman

*"Bonding is an ongoing process that begins
in pregnancy and occurs any time you recognize
the other person as a being, not an object."*

– RAHIMA BALDWIN DANCY

I never thought I would feel at home in Düsseldorf, but I did. Our apartment was on the fourth floor of a traditional Düsseldorf building located am Rhine in the Altstadt. This meant that we looked out from our living room across the Rhine River, where numerous ships carrying freight of all kinds passed by our home each day. A gray liquid highway, the river snaked between a grassy park on the far side where sheep often could be seen grazing and the generous, centuries old apartment buildings where we lived on the other. This industrial/pastoral scene was the home of various concerts, carnivals, and festivals throughout the year, all of which we could watch from the tall windows in our living room.

The evening that Coleman chose to make his entrance, September 4th, 1987, happened to be the night of the *Japanisches Feuerwerks* display. The Japanese business community, as a thanks to a partnership centered around the steel industry in Düsseldorf, planned to deliver a pyrotechnic show of fantastic proportions on the grassy banks of the Rhine directly across from our apartment.

I had been working for Esprit ever since my arrival in Düsseldorf. Having finished my day at the office, I wandered over to the local indoor *Schwimmbad*. This day the swim, which in the last week had turned into more of a slog across the shallow pool, was interrupted by a cramp at the completion of every other lap. This went on for about fifteen minutes, until I realized these cramps were actually contractions. Finally understanding I was in labor, I knew it was time to get myself packing. The contractions continued as I drove home, and by the time I had climbed the four flights of stairs to let myself into our apartment, it was all I could do to call Peter and let him know. The only thing that sounded remotely comforting was the idea of getting into the bathtub, so I did just that. Sitting cross-legged in the warm water, I rested my elbows and forehead on the cool tiles that surrounded the tub. Navigating the intensity of the contractions required my full attention. Ina May had suggested the use of visualization during this phase, so I began with the image of a wave, imagining each contraction ascending to a peak before crumbling into a deep release. It wasn't long before it felt like I was trying to swim in hurricane surf, and I knew I needed to find some other image to visualize.

The next contraction rose up with ferocity. I was alone and I had never done this before. I needed to find something that would work, something to keep me from feeling lost and becoming frightened. Just to hang on, I changed my climb up the face of a wave to that of a ladder, with every rung becoming a breath. I immediately felt much safer on a ladder than in the surf. Counting the rungs out loud (one for each breath) actually helped me to keep track of where I was and how much longer I needed to hang on before it would subside. Contractions are somewhat repetitive, so if my last "climb up the ladder" had lasted, for example, thirty-two rungs (breaths) before it began to recede, the next one would only exceed that by another breath or two. Once I knew what to expect, I didn't become overwhelmed.

It dawned on me as I was pacing myself through each contraction, that natural birth is an extremely athletic experience. It requires focus, much like running a long race or climbing a mountain. It isn't something that someone else can do for you. You are the one responsible. This experience of knowing where I was during each contraction gave me a sense of being in control, an "I can do this" feeling. Breathing my way up and down one ladder after another, I waited for Peter to arrive.

Crowds gathered in the street outside of our apartment, anticipating the fireworks. It had been closed to all cars and had become filled with a sea of spectators. By the time Peter and Dr. Djalali were able to find their way through, I was still in the bathtub and well into the final stages of labor. It was then that the fireworks began. The light of one candle filled our bedroom. Moments of calm were interspersed with explosions of light coming from outside. The reds, blues, and greens of the fireworks washed over our walls, while the blasts rattled the windows in their sills. So much for the quiet birth we had imagined!

Finally, after three hours of labor, I moved from the tub to the bed. It was time to push our baby into the world. Peter supported me from behind, leaning against the head of the bed with Dr. Djalali facing me and coaching when to push. Just as the walls glowed red, you rode into the world, Coleman. In one scoop, Dr. Djalali placed you skin to skin on my chest, and you latched on to my breast. He left all three of us alone immediately after the birth, believing that the parents should have this intimate and uninterrupted time without distraction in order to experience the miracle that had just happened. We sat together in the afterglow of the experience, spellbound by you, our new baby boy. The fireworks were over, and a peacefulness filled the apartment. After half an hour, Dr. Djalali returned and instructed Peter to cut the umbilical cord. Now we were three.

Later in the evening the midwife appeared. She had been caught in traffic and was unable to make it in time for the birth. All business, she bathed you, Coleman, with a sponge and warm water, then wrapped both of us up in warm blankets. She departed after a whirlwind of tidying up and promised to return in the morning. Satiated by your first meal, you dropped into a deep slumber. Peter and I decided to join you.

This may be stating the obvious, but you don't need to know anything about babies to have one. I am not exaggerating when I say I didn't know the first thing about a newborn. I had no younger siblings and was never interested in babysitting. As a thirty-three-year-old woman, the total time I had ever even held an infant added up to less than five minutes, and that was probably only to be polite. I had forgotten that I had no real experience (except for the stack of baby books I had dutifully read) until that moment when, woken from my dreams, I heard our son's first whimpers. Prior to this, I had tried to prepare myself. I had asked the reasonable question: How often do they eat? Looking it up in one of my trusty primers, I read the statement, "Newborns may want to nurse every two hours." Every two hours? Between like what ... 8:00 a.m. and 10:00 p.m.? No. Every two hours. I was sure that these people must have their facts wrong. I mean honestly, when would you sleep? Answer: You don't.

I heard your whimpering again. I looked across at Peter, his soft snores undisturbed by you. That moment the realization arrived with alarming clarity—this was all up to me. Sure, I could wake Peter and ask him to ... what? Watch? No, this moment was all about being a mother.

I had never quite imagined the ultimate change in my identity that this new relationship would require. Up until that minute it had just been Peter and me, with the baby being a kind of project that we were both working on. It was more of an idea than a reality. This new equation was, at its fundamental root, only between myself and my child. This is not to say that Peter wasn't helpful or involved. He would have done anything and he did. But at this particular moment, it was entirely up to me.

In the soft darkness of your first night, Coleman, I welcomed you into my arms and encircled you with warmth and familiarity. Those first quiet moments together brought a new realization: I became acutely aware that I was your world, my every action leaving a lasting impression on the freshness of your new being. My voice, my facial expressions, and my attentiveness to your needs were ingredients being added directly to your soul. I knew that my responses were creating the foundation for your entire lifetime. A deep, overriding sense of responsibility welled up within me. You were the priority in my life; nothing could have mattered more. Lesson number one: Devotion.

This devotion took root during the days and nights immediately following the birth. Doctor Djalali was adamant that the mother (and father, if possible) not leave the house or the infant's side during that first week of life. He had two reasons for this. The first was that he felt it was exposing the child to too much, too fast, to bring him into the public domain when both his immune and cognitive systems were so new and fragile. The second reason was that he viewed the first week as a crucial time for deep bonding between parents and the child—a window of opportunity that could easily be lost if there was too much distraction and commotion in the household. He even discouraged visitors and phone calls, seeing them as invasions of this sacred time.

As much as we wanted to share you with the world, Coleman, we listened to Doctor Djalali. Afterwards we realized how right he had been. Had we chosen to open our door to all visitors, our attention would not have been focused so clearly on you and our new relationship to one another as parents. The moments that support a lifetime of love could have been lost answering phones and trying to entertain others. Dr. Djalali's encouragement allowed us the luxury of time—an opportunity to enjoy the birth of our new family.

# Sweet Dreams

*"Children learn what they live."*
– DOROTHY LAW NOLTE

An undercurrent of isolation ran through my early days with you, Coleman. This was a dramatic change from my pre-motherhood life in Düsseldorf. Before you appeared, my days (and nights) were filled working for Esprit. It was a job that I loved. My colleagues were mostly single, each of us working long hours to accomplish project deadlines, facilitate store openings, and contend with the demands of each new season. We all wore black, living and breathing for the fast-paced, chic world of international design. What was cool, the hippest new restaurants and stores, and cutting edge art and architecture filled our hours and our conversations.

That world dropped away from me with your arrival. Because I didn't know any other people with babies, and both of our families were living in California, I had no one to really talk to about the issues I was encountering as a new mother. In those days, long distance communication was more difficult. There was no such thing as an email or sending a text. Phone calls, though easy to make, required consideration of the nine-hour time difference that separated us from our families. To top it off, few of our friends in Düsseldorf knew about babies. They were busy with their jobs and really didn't want to spend any of their free time with an infant. I couldn't go out in the evenings and socialize the way I used to, and in truth, I no longer shared the same interests with them. They, in turn, had no idea how to help me with the new challenges of caring for a baby. For all of these reasons, Peter and I often found ourselves inventing ways to care for you.

Before your birth, we tried our best to get ready, purchasing baby clothes and a crib. I thought the crib was so beautiful. Painted an opalescent mother of pearl, it rocked easily from side to side. It was suspended over a base that rolled smoothly around with just the slightest push of my hand. The fluffy bedding awaited you. Perfectly white, it promised restful nights in spotless linens, never letting on to the fact that babies don't sleep through the night and are anything but spotless. As beautiful as it was, there it stood, unused. I had tried it once during your first week, but you felt so far away from me. Somehow the confinement of that little white nest created an unsettling sense of separation. It just didn't feel right.

Instead, we settled into bed at night with you nestled between us. You would nurse yourself into a satiated slumber, at which point I could move you to a small futon that was right next to me beside our bed. This extra square footage meant that Peter and I could spread out at night just as we had in the good old days. I could still reach over and pat you when you whimpered, either lulling you back to sleep or snuggling you next to me so you could nurse and I wouldn't have to completely wake up. Being able to touch you easily throughout the night, letting you know you weren't alone, made us all feel more comfortable.

This all felt right to me, but knowing so little regarding babies, I wondered when I would ever get a full night's sleep again. I found myself delving into various baby books, zeroing in on the "Sleeping through the Night" chapters. I wanted to believe the "let them cry" approach would work, even though in my heart the idea felt absolutely wrong. But who was I to question the experts? Anyway, I was so tired that it hurt. I was living in a bathrobe that smelled of old milk, I couldn't think straight, and I barely recognized the face I saw every other day or so in the mirror. So I tried.

I moved the crib into another room. That night I carried you, while you were still sound asleep, and settled you into the unused white nest. I patted you until your breathing became slow and rhythmic, then tiptoed back to bed. Two hours later I woke to your initial cries. Everything in me wanted to run to you, but the book instructed me to wait ten minutes and give you the chance to fall back to sleep on your own. Those may have been the worst ten minutes of my life, and I knew they were the worst you had ever experienced. Your cries escalated from a whimper to loud screaming, accompanied by choking, panic-filled coughs and gasps. I couldn't stand it any longer. I ran to the crib and gathered you up in my arms. Your body was hot and heaving, your face wet with tears and drool. Slowly your panic receded as you began to nurse. The familiar smell and warmth of my skin settled you, and soon you were fast asleep beside me. Amidst the sense of relief I felt having you back in my arms, a primal anger bubbled. I was furious that I had fallen for such lousy, supposedly professional advice.

From that moment on, I vowed to myself I would follow my own instincts. Peter agreed. Our child-rearing style was going to have to be non-traditional because the expert advice wasn't working for us. I didn't have anyone else to talk to about it and so decided to depend upon my own intuition, knowing that your comfort translated into mine. The familiarity of raising you in this way was a welcome relief. By incorporating all of the good ideas we came across, Peter and I were able to improvise and respond to what was right in front of us. This is how I had always lived my life before you joined us, and mothering you in this same style felt only natural. Parenting intuitively brought with it the freedom to trust our own judgments. Suddenly, life was a lot more fun.

The next morning, with tremendous enthusiasm (and I admit, a fair share of exhaustion), I took all the baby books and tossed them firmly into the trash. This decision to keep you close to us at night was the beginning of our family bedroom. It was the solution that would become the answer to our sleeping arrangements for the next ten years, as our big bed became an island in a sea of wall-to-wall futons.

# A Lineage of Love

*"You are only as happy as your unhappiest child."*

– AUTHOR UNKNOWN

Mothering consumed everything. Nursing you day and night and responding to your every whimper took up so much time and energy that there was no opportunity for anything in the way of adventurous or artistic pursuits. Swimming in a sea of post-partum hormones, my every emotion became amplified. I tried to maintain a semblance of the "old me" while responding to our new baby's round-the-clock needs, but it wasn't really working. That part of me, the pre-motherhood self, began to pack her bags, saying something to the effect of "Let's take a break. I'll call you later." I had lots of conversations in my head with her about the plans we had previously shared. What about our idea of starting a design firm in New York City or all of those creative projects yet to be realized? Peter and I had only been married nine months; what about the exciting getaways we had imagined? She could see the writing on the wall. It was clear that those dreams and aspirations would have to wait. Wishing me all the best, she tiptoed out the door.

I remember being certain that I would continue my career after having a baby. I didn't realize that for me there was no after; at least there wouldn't be for several years. At first I just couldn't accept that fact. I was a product of the sixties; it was assumed that a woman could and should handle both a career and a family. As a young girl, I had been told that I could have it all, unlike the generations before mine where women were expected to stay at home and play a supportive role to their spouses. As often happens, the pendulum had now swung in the opposite direction. The sixties had changed all of the rules, allowing women to break free of the homemaker role and pursue a profession. In 1987, for a woman of my generation to consider devoting her days exclusively to a young family reflected a failure to take advantage of all that life could offer.

Although we were fortunate enough financially that I didn't need to get a job, choosing to stay at home with our baby didn't feel like enough. I didn't want to repeat the mistakes of earlier generations. Who would I be without my professional identity? Was I less than adequate if I couldn't handle both? Besides, I wanted to go back to work. I loved my job, and I missed that world where interesting conversations and design projects filled each day. The isolation of being a new mother was both unexpected and confining. As much as I loved you, Coleman, I longed for my old life. The world had promised that I could handle both.

That's how I found myself traveling to Italy for a project when you were only eight weeks old. Nancy, a good friend, offered to come with me and help care for you while I was working. We had first met one rainy Düsseldorf afternoon in our neighborhood cafe. She was sipping on her Milchkaffee at a table covered with yellow legal pads. I was seven months pregnant with you. A native Californian and Stanford graduate, she had married a German man, moved with him to Düsseldorf, and was working on her graduate thesis. We connected immediately, our friendship lightening the isolation we both felt from living in a foreign country. She had known you since birth and bonded with you from the start. When I told her about the offer I had received to do layout work for an upcoming catalogue, Nancy said she would be happy to take a break from her writing and accompany us to Milano.

It all seemed possible. Or so I thought. My job was to style clothing in attractive, graphic patterns for the photographer, and I found myself racing between the layouts and your hungry cries. Hurrying to you, I tried to nurse before any breast milk leaked onto my cool black dress. I expressed milk so that Nancy could feed you, but you refused the bottle. I could hear you crying as I arranged endless combinations of shirts, pants, and sweaters that matched the seasonal handbags, belts, and shoes. None of the work mattered to me. I could only think about you. With Nancy's help, I camouflaged my exhaustion from work combined with round-the-clock nursing. I also tried to suppress my longing to simply hold you in my arms.

At the end of the week, I returned home to our Düsseldorf apartment. I threw down my briefcase and fell onto the couch in a heap of tears. I found solace in nursing you, my rather bewildered Coleman. Curled up on the big brown couch with you in my arms, the choice became clear. I had a job—a job that wasn't going to go away. It didn't allow for weekends off or a fat paycheck. It wasn't chic and definitely not hip. It wasn't going to make me a worldly success, and I was not going to feel validated by my feminist ideals. I had to let go of all the ideas about what my life should be. I could not abandon you, this little soul whom we had invited into our lives. Not now, not yet. Not ever.

It was such a powerful realization that I sat upright on the couch. I wanted to put you first. In order to do this right, I needed to learn to accept the moment just as it was, imperfect with loose ends and unmet expectations. It was time to stop being so critical and judgmental of myself. Your appearance altered what I had previously imagined to be the course of my life and life's work. I was in completely new territory, and acceptance was clearly the best approach. The kitchen might be a mess, the bed unmade, the career on hold. Those all became distant concerns when compared to your needs. When you were happy, so was I.

Even though I wasn't a natural "baby-person," I found myself swept into the role by a force beyond choice. Perhaps it was born from the experience of being loved so thoroughly by my own mother. Hindsight nuances our understanding of the present, and as a new mother, I leaned into the memory of the love I received as a child. I wanted to pass that same experience on to you. I wanted to continue that lineage of love. This desire allowed me to consciously embrace the role of motherhood with all of my heart, despite the fact that it meant putting other parts of myself on the back burner.

I took a deep breath and intentionally exhaled (almost) everything that was getting in the way of truly experiencing peace with this decision. All of the self-imposed expectations that had kept me from fully relaxing into what was right in front of me began to dissolve. I inhaled all of the love I felt for you. Exhaling, I took all of that love and surrounded you with it. A few more breaths like this and a stillness entered my being. My jaw relaxed and my shoulders dropped. The nagging judgments released their grip. My priority became you.

To create a balanced life, I needed to attend to the necessities of each day. A new baby needs its mother. I needed community. While I might not immediately be able to return to work, I could certainly keep you with me and engage in all of the daily tasks of life that kept us both from being isolated. Shopping in the outdoor markets, visiting friends, taking daily walks along the river, teaching you how to swim, cooking together, and of course playing would fill our days. A deep wave of both loss and well-being washed over me. I switched you to the other breast.

# In Arms

*"Once we fully recognize the consequences of our treatment*
*of babies, children, one another and ourselves, and learn*
*to respect the real character of our species, we cannot fail to*
*discover a great deal more of our potential for joy."*

– JEAN LIEDLOFF

Balinese babies do not touch the ground for the first six months
of life. Instead, they are passed from person to person. After this
time a special ceremony is held, and then babies are welcome
to play on the ground. I was familiar with this practice of carrying
infants, but the idea had always sounded romantic and somewhat
impossible to replicate in our culture. In the Western world, babies
are usually confined to play pens, strollers, and cribs. This is what almost everyone did, so I assumed it was an acceptable approach. Even
so, there was something about holding a newborn being that simply
sounded like the right thing to do.

It was during this time that a friend gave us *The Continuum
Concept* by Jean Liedloff, which dramatically influenced how we par-
ented you during your first months of life. Leidloff, having lived for extended periods of time in a South American jungle with the Tauripan
Indians, noted that "The children were uniformly well-behaved: they
never fought, were never punished, always obeyed happily and instantly." This description grabbed our attention. It certainly captured the

kind of feeling that Peter and I were hoping to cultivate within our new family, but how was it done? As it turns out, the answer is not very complicated, but it is time consuming. To understand the logic of the continuum approach, it is necessary to consider the living arrangement for babies in utero: it's obvious that they have everything they require. The relationship between a mother and child during this time is a seamless one, with the natural process of pregnancy providing the child an environment of wholeness where every need is met without hesitation. The baby, long before birth, is used to being with the mother in all of her various environments. It hears the noises of the outside world, feels the rhythm of her day, her breath, and even her emotions. This is the original home of the infant. Before being born, it has only known a perfect world.

When viewed in this way, it makes sense that after the shock of birth, parents would provide this same kind of intimate and constant presence. Liedloff calls this the "in arms" phase, one that she says should be maintained until the baby begins to crawl. During this time, the newborn remains as close as possible to the parents as well as other members of the family, literally in their arms. All of the infant's needs are met without hesitation, nursing whenever the baby signals that he is hungry and soothing him before tears are shed. Through these social exchanges, the baby learns that he is a being in dialogue with others, and that if he sends signals, they will most likely be received. He experiences the world as a collection of these dialogues and trusts that when he has a need, it will be met. Being carried everywhere, either in a sling, backpack, or in arms, he becomes a part of his parents' daily life and finds stability and comfort in the rhythm of physical contact. He feels the pattern of day and night through this inclusion, which allows him the proper stimulation, free from longing and separation. Responding in this way to an infant's needs lets him know that he is lovable, worthy, and welcome.

Liedloff explains that if one allows the infant to feel "safe, wanted and 'at home' in the midst of activity before he can think, his view of later experiences will be very distinct in character from those of a child who feels unwelcome, unstimulated by the experiences he has missed, and accustomed to living in a state of want, though the later experiences may be identical." This explanation described a style of parenting that made absolute sense to us. If a being's first experience of individuation, those six months following birth, is a secure one supported by a web of attuned relationships where he feels safe, then the other benchmarks of individuation would likely follow the same pattern. David Brooks explains the importance of attachment parenting in his book, *The Social Animal,* this way:

> There is a mountain of research, known as attachment theory, which explores how different types of attachment are related to different parenting styles, and how strongly childhood attachments shape relationships and accomplishments over the course of a lifetime. It turns out that attachment, even at age one, correlates reasonably well with how people do in school, how they will fare in life and how they will develop relationships later in life. ... Securely attached children have parents that are attuned to their desires and mirror their moods. These children do not have perfect parents or perfect relationships. Children are not fragile. Their parents can screw up, lose their tempers, and sometimes ignore their children's needs, and yet if the overall pattern of care is reliable, then their kids will still feel secure in their presence.

Peter and I knew that if Liedloff's statement was true, your infancy offered a precious window of opportunity during which we could reinforce the sense of belonging with which you, Coleman, had entered the world. It was another one of those decisions that felt so right that even in our exhausted state we could embrace it fully. We chose to raise a continuum infant, deciding that until you began to voluntarily crawl, we would keep you close at all times, preferably in arms. Wearing you in a baby sling, our everyday tasks became your daily adventures and allowed for an ease of nursing so crying was unnecessary. Carrying you on my back or my hip, I was able to avoid isolation and get out of the house while still parenting in the style that felt right. When we went to the market, we filled the stroller with groceries and wore you. We found ways of doing all of the housework and cooking without putting you down. Together, you and Peter would take long walks when I needed a break. Our woven Moses basket was a helpful alternative to the sling when we wanted to lull you to sleep. It was a perfect little bed for you that was easy to travel with and allowed you to stretch out. We could bring you with us wherever we were going, and you could sleep comfortably. If you awoke, a few swings of the basket would usually send you back to dreamland. You were always with us.

Slowly everything began to make sense: the family bedroom, nursing on demand, and avoiding unnecessary tears by being together. This style of parenting required everything we had to give in the way of time and attention, but the payoff was enormous. While I have seen that love can heal anyone at any age, and no one is locked into any destiny determined by his or her childhood, receiving this in arms approach during your infancy did create an unwavering bond of trust between us. You experienced the world as a welcoming place. You rarely cried, threw a tantrum, or acted out. It established a foundation that continued through your later years and allowed you to navigate the complexities of individuation relatively smoothly, as Liedloff had described. This was especially noticeable during that period of your life labeled the Terrible Twos by the baby books, which offered advice on how to respond to tantrums and fits of aggression by the young child. But we never had these experiences with any of you and ended up calling those years the Terrific Twos, because they were.

In her book, Liedloff also describes the independence and capability of the young Tauripan children. At an early age they are allowed to venture out on their own, often with a machete in hand, exploring the jungle that surrounds them. Liedloff noticed that their parents, while always attentive, were never restrictive regarding their play, despite how dangerous it might appear. The result was that the children knew how to handle themselves with confidence. When you were small, we decided to take this same approach. We avoided words of warning such as "Watch out!" or "You'll hurt yourself!" We wanted you to take responsibility for your actions and know your own limitations. So when you were teetering on the top rung of a ladder, we might just say, "Remember, one hand for holding on," or "Plant your feet firmly." We chose to let you discover your own limits through play and exploration. We intentionally avoided making pitying sounds or racing to your rescue when you took a tumble while learning to walk. Getting your feet back under you and trying again, you learned to trust your own faculties, free from the need for reassurance. Following Liedloff's advice, we cultivated a style of parenting during these early years that included complete attentiveness to your needs, while at the same time allowing you the freedom to experience the world. This approach would remain our basic style of parenting throughout the years to come. Accidents happened and there were trips to the emergency room for stitches and the occasional cast, but what always remained intact was your sense of competency and self-confidence.

Looking back, it certainly feels like those first six months of providing an in arms experience for each of you helped to establish the closeness and trust we share with one another. The in arms approach was couched in our love for you, our belief in your basic goodness, and the understanding that children learn by the behavior modeled around them. It is the thousand small acts that build relationship. The sharing of meals as well as adventures, listening to concerns, responding with kindness, a loving touch at just the right moment—these thousand small acts support and sustain the positive bonds of family.

# Woods

In utero, Coleman weathered a Costa Rican river adventure with class five rapids and having his sleep cycle turned upside down by monthly business trips between California and Germany. He endured all-nighters putting together store openings and my love of wild dancing at late-night parties. Despite all of this, he was born with a serenity of spirit that has never left him. Woods is another being altogether. Without knowing if I had a boy or a girl, I knew that the child inside of me had a passionate character with boundless energy. Where Coleman had decided to take his time (he arrived a month after the expected due date), Woods was literally kicking to get out. He tried to make an appearance two months earlier while we were on a sailboat, but fortunately Peter and I were able to convince him otherwise. Before having children, I had always thought that a being's personal expression began with his or her first breath. I gained a deeper understanding during my pregnancy with Woods, a year after Coleman was born. In reflecting on each of your distinct personalities, I now see that you were already expressing your individual selves during both the pregnancy and the birth.

May 2nd, 1989, was an uncharacteristically sunny day in Düsseldorf. Coleman and I were about to embark on our daily excursion to
the public pool when Woods let us know that he couldn't wait any
longer. As I was closing the apartment door behind us, I was gripped
by a massive contraction. I found myself sitting in the stairwell while
Coleman, securely in the backpack, patted my shoulder. I called downstairs to our friend Uschi, a young German woman who lived beneath
us and helped to babysit Coleman. I told her that the baby was definitely on its way and asked if she would let Peter know.

I crawled back into the apartment on my hands and knees, Coleman hanging on with both arms. Once again, the bathtub called to me
as the place of maximum comfort. Coleman and I shed our clothes before the next contraction could take hold and climbed into the tub. I
turned on a soothing flow of warm water and oriented myself by once
again breathing up and down the ladder of contractions. Coleman
played with a rubber duck. Now a year and a half, he knew that the
baby would be coming any day and was happy to be keeping me company. Dr. Djalali had explained to us the importance of having siblings
present at the birth. Experiencing the new baby coming from their
mother allowed them to accept the newcomer more easily. He told us,
"Coleman won't think that you just picked it up at the market." I was
happy to have Coleman's company, and he did his best to help. When
Peter came in the door, he jumped out of the tub and ran to him, explaining all that had transpired. He brought me water during the very
active labor and sat patiently beside me while waiting for the birth. He
even picked out the first clothes that Woods would wear.

Woods, you were born half an hour later, at 10:30 in the morning,
barely waiting for Dr. Djalali to arrive. You had long, blond hair and
bright blue eyes. As was his way, the doctor placed you directly onto
my chest, the umbilical cord still connected. He then quickly herded
Uschi and the midwife out of the room, leaving Coleman, Peter, you,
and me alone together. Dr. Djalali helped us to protect the moments

immediately following your birth. Rather than having you taken from us to be weighed, cleaned, or checked, he allowed us this time to simply be. The flurry of the delivery dissolved into the peaceful wonder and enjoyment of meeting this new member of our family. I have heard it said that being in the presence of both birth and death is a holy experience. Resting in those precious moments together was indeed a sacred event.

A short time later, Dr. Djalali returned and showed Coleman how to cut the umbilical cord. Woods, you nursed happily while the morning sun poured in through the tall windows, warming the room and our skin as it filled the bedroom with light. Next to the bed, a vase of long-stemmed apricot tulips announced spring's abundance. You stopped nursing and looked around the room at all of us. Quite unexpectedly, a big smile appeared on your face. We all started laughing, which made you smile even more and then shiver with a kind of delight. Your happiness was tangible. You arrived into this world with a sense of humor and an easy presence. Your being effortlessly emanates light and brings joy to those around you. You were born this way.

Entering into your blue gaze, I fell in love with your brightness of spirit and experienced the bonding that lasts a lifetime. Peter put on a Willie Nelson song, and the lyrics floated into the bedroom—"Blue skies, smilin' at me. Nothin' but blue skies, do I see." Blue eyes, blue skies, and smiles; you brought them all.

# Lake

*"Nighttime parent-infant co-sleeping during
at least the first year of life is the universal,
species-wide normative context for infant sleep,
to which parents and infants are biologically
and psychosocially adapted. Solitary infant sleep
is an exceedingly recent, novel, and alien experience
for the human infant."*

– DR. JAMES MCKENNA

I burst into tears when I found out I was pregnant again. With an eight-month-old Woods and a two-year-old Coleman, life was so full I often felt I had lived an entire day before ten in the morning. The idea of adding one more need to the daily (and nightly) routine was unimaginable. I called my mother, who has raised eight children (three were her grandchildren), and she calmed me with the wisdom that comes from a lifetime of mothering. "Don't worry," she said. "It will be great to have them all close in age. You can do everything with them together!" I heard the truth in her words and somehow, for the first time, could imagine life with three babies. Peter and I bought another futon and awaited the new arrival.

The desire to return to the States and raise our family had brought us home to Northern California shortly after Woods's birth. We settled into our new home, delighted (after so many years of apartment living) by the idea of being able to open the kitchen door and step into an overgrown garden. Our new home in Mill Valley had an unusual floor plan, having been originally built as a one-room cottage in 1910 and then added onto by each successive owner. With one big bedroom upstairs, it worked perfectly for our family bedroom style of sleeping, and we easily moved into the oddly configured house, turning the downstairs bedroom into a communal playroom where each of you had a corner for your special treasures.

Finding a doctor in our new home was proving difficult. Fortunately, Dr. Djalali and his family had wanted to take a summer vacation in California, so we asked if they would come and stay with us, hoping the baby would arrive during their visit. Peter and I were feeling a bit more confident in our birthing skills, but we still didn't really want to go it alone. Certain that our new addition would make its appearance at any moment, we were relieved when the Djalali family finally arrived. As it turned out, Lake was in no hurry.

The days passed, and we tried to entertain our very patient guests. Their holiday was drawing to a close, yet there was still no sign of a baby ready to be born. It was Thursday, so I headed off to the farmer's market with both of you boys to pick up some summer produce. For some reason we were actually considering adopting a puppy, and I was in conversation at the ASPCA booth when I found myself doubled over with a contraction. The dog would have to wait.

We made it home, and once again the idea of getting into water sounded just right. This time we all tumbled into the pool. The cool water helped ease the passing contractions, and I could shake out the tension by swimming back and forth in between each one. Both of you paddled beside me, your water wings helping you to stay afloat. Meanwhile, Peter was desperately trying to find Dr. Djalali and his family who had left that morning for the Natural History Museum in Golden Gate Park. It was still pre-cell phone era, and he miraculously tracked them down by describing them to the security guards as a couple and two children, all dressed in white.

When he arrived, Dr. Djalali looked at me and said, "The baby is ready to come. Do you want to have it in the pool or in the bedroom?" Thinking that our bed would be more comfortable after the birth, I decided to make my way upstairs to the bedroom between contractions. Once we were settled, the boys and Peter sat beside me. We had a clear, leaded-glass window in the room that created rainbows over all of us while Dr. Djalali helped to pace the pushing. Lake, you came out in a swoosh and were a deep shade of blue, the cord wrapped tightly around your neck. This was something we hadn't anticipated. It was a frightening moment. Our new baby looked like it was hovering between life and death. I could feel Peter's arms around me, a constant support during that endless moment of uncertainty. With one swift motion, Dr. Djalali unwound the cord and you gasped. With each successive breath you regained the color in your face and then began to nurse. We were all deeply relieved.

It was at this moment that I made an observational error. For the entire pregnancy we didn't know if we were going to have a boy or a girl. We were determined not to have a preference and to welcome our new baby without a moment's hesitation. Knowing this would be our last child, it was tempting to want a girl. But more than anything we wanted our new baby to be healthy. Preference beyond that did not feel appropriate; we would certainly welcome another son. Perhaps for that very reason (along with the drama of your first breath), in the moment you arrived, Lake, I mistook the umbilical cord for a penis and thought you were a boy. I announced this to everyone as the doctor laid you on my chest. This was another one of those Dr. Djalali moments. He knew the baby was a girl but felt strongly that the parents should be the first ones to recognize the sex of the child. Everybody believed me, so when Peter, the boys, and I were left alone with you, we admired your beautiful face but were surprised at how small you were—how fine your fingers, how long and thin your limbs....

Half an hour later, Dr. Djalali came in and said, "So, how is the baby?"

"He's really different—wonderful—but not like the other two," I said.

"Are you sure it's a 'he'?" he asked.

Peter and I looked at each other, slightly shocked, and then lifted the blanket off to double check.

"A girl!" Tears streamed down both of our faces. It had been a difficult and confusing beginning. Witnessing our child unable to breathe was terrifying. The tremendous relief of the baby turning pink and then the confusion and finally excitement of her being a girl—it was a dizzying experience. We all took deep breaths, released our worries, and allowed a calm to enter the room. We landed in the moment with our healthy baby girl. Looking into your eyes, Peter and I welcomed you as our daughter. We gave you your name, Mimi Lake Buckley. It was Peter's idea to include the name "Mimi," a name I inherited because I was born on the same day as my Mother's sister, Mimi. I have always loved my aunt. It was an honor to be named after her, so I agreed. Coleman cut your umbilical cord, and we buried your placenta under a Gertrude Jekyll rosebush. To this day, it bears the most fragrant roses in the garden.

From you, Lake, I have learned what a blessing it is to have a daughter. Throughout our time together, I have felt deeply accompanied by your feminine presence. You balanced out the energetics of our home and brought a unique emotional sensitivity and kindness to every situation. Today, when I look at you, I see a beautiful young woman. Your youthful radiance has allowed me to more easily accept my own aging process. I experience through you that which I once had, and it becomes a healing continuum. This inheritance passed from mother to daughter has made the transition to the next chapters in life easier. I can release my youth with the knowledge that it lives on in you. Our intimate friendship as adults means we share a feminine perspective on the world with all of its interest and complexity. You make me feel included. This is the blessing from daughter to mother.

It was a warm summer's evening on August 16th, 1990, when you were born into our lives. Having already established our family bedroom, the nights became a curious blend of sleeping with whoever needed consolation or a snack. If any of you woke up, we could easily come and comfort you. The moments we spent with you during these nocturnal connections were equal in value to any that we could or would spend together during daylight hours. Often it was the only opportunity to be with each of you individually, as one-on-one interactions were rare. This felt like a gift of time. Peter and I had the ability to answer each of your needs equally, while also cultivating our relationship with you in the most intimate way possible. It allowed you the experience of being part of a whole, with no requirement to individuate until you were ready. This continuous relationship between all of us supported both our love for you and the love you shared with one another. In regards to the intimacy between Peter and me, we were able to maintain it in an appropriate and private way so it didn't infringe on the family bedroom. We planned "date nights" and organized occasional romantic getaways once you were old enough to be left with a babysitter. Sometimes we actually managed not to fall asleep while putting you to bed, and we ended up with an uninterrupted evening all to ourselves while you slept soundly upstairs. It wasn't always easy, and there were plenty of nights during those years when we felt both sleep and sex deprived. Still, the overall experience was one of true contentment. It definitely is not the answer for everyone, but it certainly was for us.

PART TWO

# HOME MOVIES

# Kindness is Everything

*"Be kind whenever possible. It is always possible."*
— HIS HOLINESS THE DALAI LAMA

Becoming a parent is a humbling experience. It has always seemed unfair, or at the very least a poor design, that the most difficult moments in a young marriage appear with the arrival of a baby. Just when you're learning how to relate to this other adult, an infant who requires all of your attention comes along. Of course there is the joy of having a child along with all the love you hold for that precious new being. But there are equally real challenges. These include communicating with your spouse while cultivating your new roles as parents, as well as adjusting to the schedule of the baby and accepting all that comes with it: sleep deprivation, postpartum swings of emotion, and a general feeling that there just isn't enough time in the day to get everything (or anything) accomplished.

In our new family of five, three members were in diapers. Even at these early ages, you picked up on every emotional nuance between Peter and me. You were like little satellite dishes. Whether it was our tone of voice, facial expression, or body language, you knew and responded to the emotional tenor between us. Any tension, spoken or not, you perceived. We realized pretty quickly that we had to figure out some new communication strategies because the ways we were expressing ourselves created stress.

Learning how to articulate our needs and fears before they blossomed into blame wasn't easy. Taking care of you was what we wanted to do more than anything else, but it often left Peter and me so tired that we would become irritable with one another. A normal day did not offer any time to slip away together and figure things out; there was always something that needed doing. In fact, there was so much going on that we could bury our frustrations in busyness. Of course this approach never worked, as it just meant the next conflict was fueled by old, unresolved emotions. Even though we were giving it our all, the addition of three babies to our young marriage became an emotional challenge.

Up to that point in our lives, if a relationship became difficult, we could simply leave it. Being parents changed that equation and gave reason to the relationship beyond ourselves. We wanted it to work. We wanted to build a family together. Our focus was on keeping our marriage vibrant and our communication both kind and authentic. Knowing we were in it for the long haul, we began to look for answers to our issues. We certainly weren't the first couple to face this challenge. Admitting we needed to learn some new skills, we decided to ask for help. That's how Seymour came into our lives. His first words upon hearing our story were, "Divorce is not an option." This shocked us. We certainly weren't even close to thinking of divorce as a possible solution. It was the last thing either Peter or I wanted. However, by taking it off the plate so completely, it freed us to focus on the present and the issues in front of us. With the clear priority of making a happy and fulfilling life together, it became easier to stop pointing fingers and begin to really listen to one another.

Seymour's wise and kindly presence, more like a grandfather than a therapist, calmed us. He described what he called "our two brains": the primitive limbic system and our more evolved and wiser cortical and neocortical system. In his book, *Who's Talking Now,* he explains that "the limbic system impulses travel many times faster than the neocortical impulses. The result is that the limbic system highjacks the thought process because it initiates action based on its agenda before the neo-cortical has a chance to respond wisely."

The limbic alarms are easily recognized by their accompanying responses of fight, flight, or freeze. Yelling, pouting, or stomping away are the symptoms of our limbic brain. I was particularly good at flight, while Peter specialized in sticking around for a fight. The problem with this was that I would get frightened when Peter sounded angry, and he would feel frightened when I abandoned him by disappearing emotionally. Seymour explained to us that the *fear* of not having our needs met was at the root of every argument. When we unintentionally and unknowingly frightened one another, it was because old fears, often from childhood, would become triggered. To learn how not to do this, Peter and I had to cultivate an understanding of our own, as well as each other's, emotional history. This process was difficult at times as we acknowledged painful memories. But in witnessing each other's stories, a new empathy grew between us and allowed us to understand one another's struggles. Seymour called this work *cleaning out the basement* and assured us it was essential if we wanted to learn how to relate without setting off limbic responses that could result in destructive exchanges.

A few tricks Seymour taught us to help defuse the moment when fear took hold included beginning a potentially difficult conversation with the phrase, "I feel frightened...." It might be something as simple as my saying to Peter, "I feel frightened driving at this speed. Would you please help me feel better by slowing down?" My father was a maniac behind the wheel, and my childhood memories of his crazy driving still make my heart race. Learning to identify our fears allowed us to recognize the real source of our upset, and it usually had little to do with the other person. This understanding helped me to avoid the pre-Seymour response of "Slow down! You're driving too fast!" which would certainly have triggered Peter's highly attuned early childhood fear of criticism, and the fight would be on. If for whatever reason we still landed ourselves in combative territory, we would call a time out and let our emotions settle before trying to resolve things. Above all, apologies were always accepted.

In addition, Peter and I would plan a great escape every six months or so. In a perfect world, all young parents would have the opportunity to take time off together. Once, and sometimes twice a year, we would carve out two entire days and nights for ourselves, leaving you with a babysitter that everyone liked. During these getaways we were able to be with each other free from any responsibilities other than that of re-connecting. We had time for conversations, reflections, and even dis-agreements without interruption from the ringing phone or the needs of daily life. We remembered why we loved each other and marveled at all that had happened so far in our marriage. Returning home rested and in love was the best gift we could possibly give to you.

Along with learning how to care for our relationship, we needed to help you develop your own communication skills. I will always remem-ber the moment we decided to insist on kindness in our family. Peter was in the kitchen with Coleman and Woods when you were two and three years old. He tells the story this way:

> We were sitting together playing on the floor when all of a sudden Coleman hit Woods pretty hard. I was sitting right next to them, and before I had any time to think, my hand snaked out and hit Coleman. I had never hit Coleman before, and I never have since, but it went so fast there was no think-ing about it. Coleman had such a look of shock on his face that I felt I owed him an explanation, and in fact, I needed to figure it out myself. I told Coleman that fathers care more about their children than anything in the world. If anyone tried to hurt him, I would protect him 'like an angry lion.' There is something about being a father that makes you will-ing to fight to the death for your child. It's just inside of you; it's what happens when you are a father. But Coleman, I asked, what happens when one of your own children attacks another one? A father doesn't know what to do. You want to

protect one, but you don't want to hurt the other. It's an impossible situation. I told him I was really sorry to have hit him and that I felt terrible about it. Then I asked him never to put me in that situation again because it made me unhappy and confused. Coleman seemed to grasp that hitting didn't work.

We knew Coleman wouldn't fully understand this entire explanation, but the experience brought us to the realization that we had to do something about it. After this incident, we acknowledged the need to make kindness a requirement in our family. Certainly the first step was for Peter and me to model it with one another and with each of you. Beyond that, we weren't so sure.

It was during this time that we discovered the work of Jane Nelson and her books on positive discipline, which include practical applications to help children cultivate self-discipline, responsibility, cooperation, and problem-solving skills. Grounded in respect, her approach understands a misbehaving child to be a discouraged child. Encouragement is employed as a basic motivator. Positive discipline involves exactly that: saying things in a way to avoid blame or shame. Instead of phrasing statements or requests in the negative, Nelson instructs us to express ourselves in a positive way. Before, we might have said, "Don't play so roughly with the cat!" Navigating with positive discipline, we would re-word it to be a statement such as, "Let's treat the cat gently." All of us can hear positive statements much more easily than negative ones, and speaking to children in this way is more effective. Plus, it creates a relaxed and safe atmosphere where anger can be transformed.

Experiencing the natural consequences of one's actions is inherent in positive discipline, making punishment unnecessary. In order to master this, it is essential to clarify your own expectations through teaching, modeling, and making things fun. For example, young children don't naturally know how to wipe up a mess. If something spills, rather than getting upset and telling them to clean it up, teach them how to do it. Make it an adventure to open the cupboard and find the right tools for the job. Avoiding blame, you can explain to your children how something is done so that the next time they can begin to understand how to do it for themselves. Pepper the experience with *please* and *thank you*. This is how children learn. Nelson differentiates between positive discipline and permissiveness. It is not about giving children permission to do anything they want; there are expectations and consequences. The important part is learning how to frame the situation in a positive way that maintains the child's dignity while defining boundaries and offering choices. Teaching, as well as listening, are vital components of positive discipline.

This approach felt right to us. If one of you became upset or angry, we would help you to express yourself—how you felt and what it was you needed. We encouraged you to find your own solutions by asking problem-solving questions: Can you tell me what happened? What can we do to make it better? Often it was a good idea to take some quiet time so that you could cool off, but it wasn't offered as a punishment. Rather, it was a time to think things through.

This is how we cultivated kindness in our home. Fighting and yelling weren't allowed. When conflicts arose, which they did, they would be met with a response aimed at understanding the issues involved so we could figure out how to resolve them. The expression, "Use your words" (as opposed to hitting each other) was a common one around our house. Most of the time it worked.

Requesting kindness and employing positive discipline during your early years, though challenging, was worth the effort. It is a learned behavior and required each of us to move beyond our primal, reactive responses in order to see the larger emotional picture and everyone's different needs, including our own. It didn't just happen because we wanted it to, and every exchange was not perfect, but with practice it became easier and certainly provided a positive groundwork for later interactions. It was a natural extension of the in arms phase when you knew your needs would be met. Because we cultivated positive discipline early on, when you became teenagers, it was already an established pattern of behavior. Recently I checked with each of you to see if

I remembered your adolescent years correctly. Were they really free of yelling, angry words, and tantrums? You confirmed my memories. Because we made the choice, fighting was not a necessary component of our family life.

Individuating and dealing with surging hormones, however, is a natural part of growing up. We learned when you became teens that the kind of help you really wanted was just to know that Peter and I were there and we loved you. Other than that, you usually wanted to work things out for yourselves. We were careful not to interrogate you about your feelings, knowing you would come to us if you wanted to discuss something. Adolescence is a complex time for everyone involved. The parent/child relationship requires a transformation from total reliance toward growing independence. There is a shift in the balance of power that requires emotional agility on the part of the adults. It is easy to mistake this new need for separation and personal space as a loss of connection. In fact, parenting during the teen years is just as needed as it ever was, but it does require a new perspective. One of the most helpful tools we discovered during this time was the power of childhood photographs. A teacher of yours suggested that as you all entered into the confusing realm of adolescence, we place your early childhood photos around the house. These pictures were especially helpful during the more trying moments of your teenage years, reminding Peter and me of your innate goodness and all of the loving moments we had shared with each of you. I imagine they also offered you an emotional port in the rough seas of adolescence, with memories of the simpler days of childhood. The photos reminded us that while change is a constant, so is our love for one another. Remembering this foundation, we could better resolve any issue.

# Eat Together

*"Eat food. Not too much. Mostly plants."*
– MICHAEL POLLAN

Engraved in the memory of my own childhood is a prominent grandfather clock that loomed with polished elegance in our front hall; the golden, filigreed hands pointed out the passing of our days. Its sound permeated our house, the confident chime giving count to the hours it had so carefully ticked away. Creating a recognizable rhythm within the home allows for a safe and secure atmosphere where every being can thrive, especially animals and young children. These positive boundaries are established through the repetition of daily acts such as mealtime, playtime, bedtime, bath time, and the rituals that accompany them. When experienced as a whole, home becomes a place of steady consistency where everyone can relax, confident in the certainty that needs will be met.

Mealtimes established the rhythm of my early years. Every morning when the clock struck seven, the promising scent of toast and coffee wafted through our house, accompanied by the morning ritual of newspaper reading and small conversations. Because school and work pulled everyone away from home during the day, it was only on the weekends that lunch found its rightful place. But dinner was sacred. I loved the ritual of gathering family around the dinner table. Conversations included tales of one's day, family stories, and my father's colorful jokes, all over food that was thoughtfully prepared.

As a child, my favorite place to be was in our kitchen, where real life happened. I remember sitting on the cool, yellow linoleum floor, brushing one of the lounging dogs while my mother searched through her cookbooks, making a shopping list for the evening's meal. The milkman would call out his greeting, tromping through the back door on his weekly mission to replace the empty bottles with full ones. A sink, full of breakfast dishes on one side and a riot of garden flowers waiting to be arranged on the other, was a common sight. My mother would come home from the market laden with bags full of ingredients to prepare the various dishes and begin to pull out bowls, pans, cutting boards, and platters, all humming with possibility.

The kitchen of your childhood was born from these memories. With the three of you in diapers, it was essential to keep an eye on you while carrying on with the daily tasks of life. A gift from your grandmother was my love of cooking, and since I was in the kitchen a lot, it needed to be a fun place for everyone. At a yard sale we found a toy wooden stove with pretend burners and a plastic sink, just the right size for you to stand at and "cook." Next to that, we placed a small table and three little chairs where you could sit easily without help. A big basket of pots, pans, dishes, and utensils translated into hours of imaginary play where you would serve up meals composed of flowers, shells, nuts, and rocks. Close at hand was a large art closet brimming with baskets of crayons, felt tip pens, paper, paints, brushes, scissors, tape, glue, beeswax, and felt. It was like a babysitter that did everything but clean up afterwards. Hanging over it all from an exposed wooden beam was a thickly knotted jute rope, perfect to climb on, with a soft cushion under it that doubled as a place to stretch out and nap.

Since the pantry space was taken up with art supplies, I arranged all of our produce around a tall stool placed in the corner. Draped with a colorful cloth, it was surrounded by baskets full of whatever the garden had to offer. Fall filled the corner with pumpkins, apples, cornstalks, and squashes; even the occasional scarecrow made an appearance. Summer provided us with baskets of peaches, tomatoes, apricots, and gigantic zucchini too big to eat but too beautiful for the compost. Flowers poked their heads out of the composition that included African baskets and big golden teapots. It became a seasonal altar—our version of the grandfather clock.

Appreciation for good food has been a common thread in our family from one generation to the next. Before we were married, we visited your uncle Lindley and aunt Corrine, both excellent cooks. I was impressed by their two young daughters. Your cousins, always included at every meal, would eat anything that was put in front of them. I asked Corrine how they managed to raise such adventurous eaters. She responded that it was easy; whatever they cooked for dinner was for everyone. They never differentiated except when the girls were infants. During that time, they would use a small grinder and simply mash up whatever was being served so a baby could enjoy it. The girls learned to like all kinds of food from the very beginning. We took this great advice to heart and found that it worked. It is always a good idea to create a stress-free environment around eating. Your great-grandmother began each meal with her grandchildren by saying, "Only eat the things that taste good to you." Not having to eat everything in front of us took the pressure off and made us want to try new foods and flavors. It also allowed everyone at the table to feel comfortable and at ease.

As you grew up, your cooking efforts moved from the small wooden stove to the real one. Soups made from flower petals were replaced with scrambled eggs, pancakes, and cookies of all kinds. The cutting, chopping, and peeling we did together offered opportunities for creativity as well as conversation. These simple and repetitive acts allowed a safe haven for subjects that might have otherwise stayed quietly hidden in the busyness of our lives. In the intimate world that surrounded us while shelling peas or kneading bread, incomplete thoughts and subterranean feelings could spill out and find their voices. I learned about who liked whom in the fifth grade and which teachers were the favorites. Discussions around the latest fashion trends might evolve into sharing previously unspoken worries and fears. Even if we couldn't solve these concerns completely, we were able to talk about them, which always helped. The kitchen became the heart of our home, weaving us together through the daily tasks of our culinary creations.

Over time, the small table in the kitchen disappeared, and a large oval one took its place. This became the favorite location for doing homework or the occasional art project until it was time for dinner. Papers and binders were put aside for placemats and napkins set with whatever the meal required in the way of spoons, forks, and knives. Flowers or a basket of warm bread usually sat in the midst of it all, surrounded by candles, shells, pinecones, or feathers—treasures found on recent adventures. We would share the stories of the day, catching up with your challenges, successes, and dreams. This practical celebration of mealtime grounded our lives with its daily rhythm. We found that the simple act of eating together nourished our bodies and our spirits, aligning us more deeply to one another.

# The Garden: A School at Home

*"What can educators do to foster real intelligence? . . .*
*We can attempt to teach the things that one might*
*imagine the earth would teach us: silence, humility,*
*holiness, connectedness, courtesy, beauty, celebration,*
*giving, restoration, obligation and wildness."*

– DAVID W. ORR

While finishing up dinner dishes that evening, I found myself saying to Peter, "I think we could create a really good kindergarten or at least a pre-kindergarten." Even though you were all under the age of three, I had decided to check out our options for schools. I was certain there would be any number of wonderful possibilities for early education in our enlightened community, but after a day of visiting various kindergartens and preschools, I wasn't so sure. Classrooms filled with plastic toys and exhausted teachers trying to meet the needs of twenty young children or more seemed to be the norm. There was no inherent beauty in these indoor environments and definitely no experience of peace. Outside, play spaces were mainly composed of asphalt fields broken up with generic play structures surrounded by beauty bark and the occasional sand box, home to broken trucks and pails. The children looked either anxious or frantic, and nothing about any of the seven or more schools I visited made me feel any better about sending you, Coleman, into the fray of preschool.

So, over a sink of dirty dishes, the idea of making a small school was born. It all seemed so possible, and we were blissfully unaware at the time that this idea would consume our lives for the next fifteen years. All we knew in that moment was that creating a small playgroup sounded appealing. We certainly knew other parents who would like to share in what could be a gentle start to their child's schooling. Was there a system of education we should consider? Our wise friend Anna, mother of five, advised us to look into the Waldorf approach. "Just go visit their kindergarten; you'll see what I mean."

That is how we found ourselves in the soft pink, candle-lit class-room. Neatly arranged baskets full of wooden toys sat on polished red-wood shelves alongside handcrafted dolls and animals fashioned from cotton, felt, and wool. There were velvet pillows to sit on and baskets of rainbow silks that could be draped over wooden frames to make cozy play spaces. A nature table decorated with colorful fabrics featured a tribute to the harvest season with handmade fairies dancing through an arrangement of Indian corn, pumpkins, and apples still on their leafy branches. At the round wooden table, ten children were quietly engaged in painting with watercolors. Nestled in the corner was a kitchen with a small table and chairs where the children could bake. The smell of warm oat bread wafted from the oven. Weaving together all of these threads was the teacher, who told a fairy tale she accompanied with the gentle strums of her lyre. A lyre? I could hardly believe my ears. Everything about the classroom was so inviting. We sat entranced as the soft light filtered in through pink silk curtains, giving the room a rosy glow.

The entire experience brought tears to my eyes—tears for the sensitivity of this approach, for the way it so respected and protected the wonder and delight inherent in a young child's nature, and tears for all of the children who would not or could not receive this gentle beginning. Sitting in the Waldorf kindergarten that day, listening to the singing, storytelling, and laughter, feeling the innate and intentional reverence which filled the classroom, we knew we had found the kind of education all children deserved and we wanted you to have.

We learned that Waldorf education has its roots in the spiritual/ scientific research of the Austrian scientist and thinker Rudolf Steiner (1861–1925). He saw every individual as a three-fold being of spirit, soul, and body whose capacities unfold in three developmental stages on the path to adulthood: early childhood, middle childhood, and adolescence. These stages described by Steiner gave us insight and understanding about age-appropriate activities for children, starting with kindergarten and continuing through the grades.

Although his philosophy regarding the developmental stages of a child felt significant, there were other components intrinsic to the Waldorf curriculum that might have been more appropriate in 1919 postwar Germany. This became the topic of discussion among a small group of parents who wanted the same education for their children as Peter and I did. We were a diverse group of mothers and fathers, all products of the sixties, including artists, lawyers, naturalists, and writers. What we held in common was the dream that we could create a unique educational experience for our children.

Because we did not want to be bound to the entire pantheon of Waldorf philosophy, we called ourselves a "Waldorf-inspired" school. We began by hiring Waldorf-trained teachers who agreed with our approach. As a group, we worked together to craft a mission statement describing the primary values we wanted to integrate into the existing Waldorf curriculum. These included the celebration of Universal Spirituality instead of the Christian orientation found in traditional Waldorf education. Universal Spirituality honored our interdependence and connectedness, recognizing that we are one with all of life. It viewed as sacred the earth with its seasons and daily rhythms. Our Waldorf-inspired school emphasized reverence and stewardship for the planet as viewed through the lens of deep ecology, a perspective that came after Steiner's time. In addition, we included a gender-balanced, multicultural curriculum. All of this was grounded in positive discipline, an approach that allowed parents, teachers, and children an avenue for respectful communication. We believed this revised curriculum reflected what Steiner would have supported had he lived into the twenty-first century.

Our first efforts to grow a school quickly became complicated. Finding a location was not an easy task. So when a supportive parent who was currently housing his business in an unused elementary school offered us two classrooms, we jumped at the chance. It didn't take long before we realized why so many of the classes we had visited in the beginning looked the way they did. Starting a school and running it on a budget wasn't easy. In order to afford the rent and salaries, we needed to fill the classrooms with at least twenty paying families. Because we needed students, we accepted families who were not necessarily interested in our Waldorf-inspired ideas. We opened The Mountain School in the fall of 1990 with a pre-kindergarten and a kindergarten class that each had twenty children. We had all worked hard to make it happen, and we now had much greater sympathy for the struggles other schools faced.

While the school was basically a success, Peter and I felt our initial vision had been compromised. The large classes lacked the intimacy we had imagined, and the majority of the parents were not committed to our same ideals. To top it off, Coleman, when I brought you in for your first day of school, it became very clear that it was not your cup of tea. I had convinced you to come visit the classroom by saying we needed to bring toys for the sandbox. I was sure that once you were there you would want to stay. But having dropped off the toys, you were ready to go home. When I explained I would return later, you burst into tears. In that moment your teacher, Devika, and I experienced the kind of unforgettable eye contact that makes any conversation unnecessary. You were unhappy, frightened, and you wanted to leave. You were not ready to be left in a room with twenty strangers. It was as simple as that. I held Lake in my arms while Woods watched the entire scene with concern on his face. This was not what I had imagined or expected.

Steiner supported the idea of home being the best place for the very young child. In fact, the idea behind any traditional Waldorf kindergarten (which begins when a child is five or six years old) is that it look and feel like a home, including having a kitchen. Even though you had just turned three, we thought the classroom setting would foster your social as well as your small motor skills. Were we doing you a disservice by not forcing you to stay in preschool? Would you fall behind other children your age? Driving away from the school that day, I decided to trust Steiner's perception and your gut feeling about what was best. Home did feel better.

It is easy in our culture to accelerate the childhood experience. We watch as our babies move from helpless infants into competent walkers and talkers, even before the age of two. They are curious and so much more capable than they were at birth, and as parents we want to support their development. I am certain you could have adapted to the classroom setting, Coleman. I am also certain we could have left you to cry it out in another bedroom and you would have learned to sleep through the night. But as parents, we chose another path. Rather than giving you away at such an early age, we decided to keep you at home, slow things down, and let you tell us when you were ready to join a classroom setting. We organized child care at our house so there would be uninterrupted periods of time when Peter and I could focus on other things besides the three of you. This solution worked out well for everyone. Over time, each of you expressed your own unique timing regarding readiness for school and extended social interactions. Listening to your cues made these transitions positive ones, free from tears (mine or yours!). Keeping you at home and letting each of you leave the nest when you felt truly ready allowed you to individuate in the most personal way possible, without any outside pressure.

That is how we decided to combine our home with the school experience. Although The Mountain School continued, successful in all of its efforts, we decided to start over, start small, and start it at our home on the mountain. The following year, we hired a Waldorf-trained teacher and began with a playgroup of six children from our original classes. The school day began at nine and ended at noon so that you could come down to our kitchen for lunch. As parents, we all shared similar values. We were committed to media-free childhoods, eliminating television and video games from our homes during your early years. We avoided fast or processed foods, dressed you in clothing free of corporate logos, and made respectful communication between everyone a priority. We all wanted to play an active role in our children's education as creators, not consumers. This was not an idea that appealed to everyone, but the small group of parents who showed up with their children were devoted to this project.

Our first year went so smoothly it seemed only natural to continue. Each day, Coleman, you were happy to climb the steps up to the Hummingbird House, a room above our garage we transformed into an airy abode with a kitchen, a sunny play area, and a large wooden table that could accommodate all of the various art projects. The windows looked out upon the surrounding redwoods, fruit trees, and flower garden. Tall trees nestled next to a small creek whose song filled the forest, a place you frequented often to sit in the tipi and listen to stories. The vegetable garden was an integral part of your school day, as were the inviting mountain trails that began just past our top gate.

Cultivating a strong sense of wonder is the focus of the Waldorf curriculum during the early childhood years. We embraced that idea completely. Mondays through Thursdays were full of art, music, gardening, cooking, singing, storytelling, and games, while Fridays were called Nature Day, devoted to developing your relationships to the natural world by discovering the surrounding wilderness with a naturalist.

By the next year Woods wanted to join in, and it was next to impossible to keep Lake from tagging along behind. That's how we ended up with three classes: The Ravens, The Spotted Fawns, and The Hummingbirds. With a pre-kindergarten, kindergarten, and a first grade, our playgroup had become a real school. At this point, we knew we were committed to creating a Waldorf-inspired education for the three of you and your classmates. The Garden School took root at our home and thrived there for five years.

One sunny morning in March, 1996, as the three of you were leaving the kitchen for school, a fire truck, two police cars, and a reporter appeared in our driveway. Peter and I looked at each other and knew it wasn't just a courtesy call, so we went to see what had brought these visitors. The officer in charge informed us we were not zoned to have a school on our property. We would need to close it down and hopefully find a new location where an educational facility was permitted. By this time, our community included thirty children and six teachers; we couldn't deny we had a school going on.

Actually, this news was not a huge surprise to us, as we knew we were not authorized to have a school at our home. It wasn't a problem that had stopped us; we had inherited a rebellious spirit from growing up in the sixties. For better or worse, we weren't afraid to question authority or break some rules. Besides, we really had been looking for an appropriate place to relocate, but it wasn't easy to find one. We welcomed all of the officials, who asked if they could please inspect the classrooms for safety. We agreed, feeling strangely eager to show them the school our community had created.

Not unlike our own first experience that day five years prior in the pink Waldorf kindergarten, we watched as the police, reporter, and firemen became spellbound by each classroom and the activities of the children. The kindergarten offered them bread warm from the oven and invited them to the tipi. The visitors joined the children as they sat in a circle listening to fairy tales and singing songs. The first grade met them in the garden. There they harvested potatoes, leeks, and garlic while studying butterflies with their Nature Day teacher. The second grade played several songs on their recorders and then recited a full-length fable by heart. By the end of the visit, the officials were all deeply moved by what they had experienced. They decided against closing the school, telling us instead that we needed to find a new location for the following year. Waldorf education had once again worked its magic.

The next day there was a picture in the local newspaper of Woods's class all sitting on the stairs of the Hummingbird House. The article described our school as "an intimate group of children from many walks of life (half are on scholarship) whose families have gathered around a simple educational philosophy: Growing whole beings in the natural world." Like it or not, we were growing up. The real world awaited us.

We were able to find a new home for the Garden School by the following fall in a sunny, two-story building that sat right in the heart of Mill Valley. Changing our name to the Greenwood School, we continued with the same intentions and the goal of educating you through middle school. Once again, younger siblings wanted to join in, and eventually our project became a school complete with a kindergarten through eighth grade.

Working together as a team, the parents and teachers committed to weekly Parent/Teacher Circles that helped direct the course of the school. Together we developed our educational philosophy, determined the budget, imagined our future, designed curriculum, and established school policies and procedures. We spent hours considering every detail of your experience in the classroom. Which songs to sing and stories to tell? How could we design a curriculum that each week included an entire day spent outside in nature? What was the best cure for pinworms and should it be mandatory? Was it really acceptable that you weren't expected to read until third grade? Could we leave the word God out of the curriculum, replacing that concept with the understanding that all of life is seamlessly interconnected? Were computers acceptable after sixth grade? Should we continue to avoid standardized testing? Was teaching electric guitar in our strings program appropriate? Should the girls be able to wear make-up and the boys dye their hair? These were some of the questions we faced while trying to keep our little school on track.

As we grew, we hired an administrator to handle the daily tasks of answering phones, organizing billing, and keeping up with correspondence. We expanded our governance to include a finance committee, hiring committee, and faculty committee. My favorite was the festival committee, a group of parents who oversaw all of our seasonal celebrations. During these occasions our entire community would gather together, enjoying the performances put on by each of your classes which often included singing, dancing, playing instruments, and recitations of poetry. Afterwards we would share a vegetarian potluck feast, each family bringing a contribution that reflected the offerings of that particular season. Large golden teapots of hot ginger tea always accompanied these gatherings along with another favorite: Cho's Special Noodles.

As parents, we took complete responsibility for educating all of you. This often felt like we were reinventing the wheel, because while our teachers had received Waldorf training, none of the parents had any previous experience in creating a school. We really didn't want to make any big mistakes. Running a school, however, is a complex and challenging endeavor with a seemingly endless parade of problems to be solved. Conflicts would arise. We had constant debates over what was meant by Waldorf-inspired, how to fill classes, and how to best serve those children with learning differences. We also dealt with the occasional unhappy parent or teacher and the daily job of trying to keep the seventh grade girls from wearing revealing outfits. Even with these ups and downs, we were able to keep the growing community intact and our love for the school alive. The aesthetics inherent in the classroom environment and the breadth of the curriculum were a constant inspiration, fueling our enthusiasm for this unique education and the opportunities it offered.

Creating a school for you required a tremendous amount of time, hard work, and perseverance over fifteen years. All of the parents and teachers involved devoted themselves to making the most intentional and beautiful learning experience possible. This effort came with its fair share of anxious moments and conflicting viewpoints. To help prevent factions from forming, we incorporated a kind of decision making known as concordance. This approach, brought to us by one of the parents, a professional facilitator, involved stating aloud a clear proposal to solve the issue at hand. We would then go around the room and each person could say either yes or no to it. After hearing from everyone, we would then make a second pass to hear the reasons for the no's. In addition, if any of the original yes votes sounded even slightly hesitant or tinged with a shred of doubt, we would ask those individuals what concerned them about the original proposal. Often we would have to repeat this process several times, knowing we could not make any decision that wasn't completely agreed upon by everyone. This slowed down our decision-making process, which wasn't always a bad thing. It also meant that once we did come to an agreement, we did it as a group. No one felt left out or unheard. Because of concordance, we all ended up on the same side of the fence. It was a powerful tool for maintaining a healthy and harmonious atmosphere within the school.

Being involved on a personal level with your education was deeply rewarding. As in all acts of service, we were also served. In my case, I realized the intensely academic education I received in my early years lacked an understanding of the young child's developmental capacities. As an adult, it was healing to create an educational experience for you that was so responsive and appropriate to your needs. We like to think you benefitted from it as well and saw it as an expression of our love for you, even if it was, after all, still school.

# Celebrate

We wanted you to fall in love. Maybe it would be with a snap pea, a raspberry, or perhaps a basil leaf wrapped around a cherry tomato. It could be with the Chiogga beet's stripes or the size of a forgotten zucchini at the end of summer. Whatever it was, we wanted you to fall in love.

It all began with making beds. Together we would sink sharp shovels into the dirt, loosening damp clods woven with roots from last season. Cracking open the brown crust might reveal a surprised earthworm flailing half in, half out. Excited cries of discovery filled the air when pill bugs scattered from their cozy home underneath an old pumpkin. The trowels were the perfect tool for you. Loosening the soil, now crumbling and warmed by spring sunshine, surrounded us all with the fresh smell of dirt. After a morning of preparation, the sifting of the soft, dark beds was complete.

Peter, having pored over seed catalogues during the winter months, had carefully chosen heirloom varieties of vegetables that would not only taste good but were somehow unique—purple tomatoes, red okra, giant pumpkins, and decorative gourds that looked like swans. Opening the seed packets, each one illustrated with its own promising outcome, we began to plant. Cupped hands welcomed the round seeds.

70

Your fingers poked holes just deep enough to put in one small miracle. Then covering it carefully with a blanket of dirt, you patted it to sleep. Wait and see, we said. Wait and see.

Raincoats and muddy rubber boots were left at the kitchen door, and while the seeds slept tightly in the dark, we thought about other things like coloring eggs and tie-dying everything in the house that was white. Time passed. The morning sun filled our bedroom with a new kind of brightness since the equinox. The rooster announced another day. It was so much easier to get up, now that the mornings weren't dark and cold. Racing downstairs, you decided to visit the chickens and check for eggs while Peter made waffles.

We could hear your shouts from the kitchen. "They've woken up! The peas are awake!" We came out to see the three of you examining a row of small green leaves, newly unfurled. Next to the peas, wiggly rows of radishes appeared. Lettuces and beets poked up as well, joined by zucchinis and pumpkins safe in their raised beds. The love affair had begun.

It is easy to celebrate something you cherish. We would join together with everyone in the school to create seasonal festivals, each with its own traditions. These events marked in a memorable way the rhythms of the earth and the annual cycles that so deeply affect our lives. Recognizing these planetary transitions allowed us to understand the emotional states that accompany them: the buoyancy of springtime, the outwardness of summer, collecting ourselves at harvest, and the cozy inwardness of winter. By acknowledging and celebrating each season, we also experienced the undeniable interrelationship between ourselves and the earth.

We knew spring was near when the bare limbs of our cherry tree became lost in a pink cloud of blossoms. In anticipation of the Spring Festival, you would each fill a straw basket with a layer of soil, just enough for a handful of wheat berries to take root. You then added another layer of the rich dirt, pressing it down so the berries were nestled in place. After watering, the baskets were lined up against a sunny wall. Two weeks later they finally sprouted—soft green beds for the treasures of the egg hunt. Most of the eggs were made in your classrooms or at home. Some were hand blown, shimmering with golden paint and beads, while others were dyed in layers of pastel hues. Still others were made of chocolate, popcorn, sugar, rubber, chalk, and soap. Always included were the candle eggs, decorated by the parents with thin sheets of colorful beeswax. Everyone loved the egg hunt because it wasn't competitive. Before the hunt began, you children were shown the twelve different eggs you needed to find. You would then run out to the garden, baskets in hand, to find your set of twelve. The older children usually found their dozen first and would return to the hunt to help the younger ones complete their baskets. At the end of the day everyone went home with the same collection of treasures.

The next month we raised the Maypole's fluttering ribbons. Dancing in our colorful clothing, wearing crowns of flowers under the budding trees, we wove a rainbow-hued pattern around the gnarled redwood pole to the tunes of fiddle and guitar. May baskets brimming with lilac, pink jasmine, baby roses, and daffodils, all picked that morning from our gardens, were exchanged as gifts. Occasionally the Green Man, dressed in green shorts and vines, would make an appearance. This visitation always surprised our May Queen—a role assumed by whoever was pregnant at the time. Part of the day's festivities included planting a Japanese maple. Throughout the seasons you saw the leaves change color, drop, and reappear. Years passed, allowing you to mark the tree's growth with your own.

Fall brought the Harvest Festival complete with everyone in homemade costumes, a cast of characters that often included fairies, wizards, the Bubble Wrap Man, and a Blessing in Disguise. Within a large fairy ring of redwoods, pumpkins and sunflowers surrounded the wooden altar where photos of deceased loved ones were accompanied by the glow of candles—a remembrance of our ancestors and the passing of time. Our garden, once green, now had turned golden, reflecting this natural cycle of life.

When the days grew shorter, we planted narcissus bulbs, made paper lanterns, and prepared for the Evergreen Spiral, a festival celebrating the light within the darkness of winter. The evening gathering began, illuminated only by a tall, red candle that sat in the center of a spiral made from evergreen boughs. All of you children, dressed in your finest, would walk individually into the heart of the spiral. From the flame of the center candle, you would light your small golden one, which sat securely in a polished red apple. Retracing your steps, you placed your candle amongst the boughs. By the end of the ceremony, our spiral filled the room with a galaxy of light.

These gatherings strengthened our community and oriented us toward the natural rhythms of the earth. Celebrating what we loved, these larger festivals often translated into smaller celebrations within our home, usually invented by the three of you. One in particular comes to mind:

It was summer, and the peas were now well over our heads, their green tendrils clinging to the netting hung against the warm, stone wall. It was harvest time, and Granny was visiting. Coleman came bursting into the kitchen, his face bright with excitement.

"Granny! Come on down to the garden! We're having a pea-party!"

As we made our way down the grassy path, we saw on the lawn below us a green and white checkered tablecloth neatly spread out under the shade of the persimmon tree. At each setting, a small white bowl brimmed with newly picked peapods. You were all sitting in your places waiting for us so that the party could begin. We settled ourselves down in the grass and snapped open the bright green skins, home to the sweet-tasting sugar snap pea. Afterwards we all agreed—let's do it again next year.

All of these seasonal festivals and rituals shared a common thread: They were each an expression of gratitude for the earth and an acknowledgement of all it offers. We celebrated each season in the company of family and friends, thus deepening the bonds we shared with one another. Taking this time to come together and notice the natural world allowed us to fall even more deeply in love with this planet and the miracle of life. Cultivating and strengthening this relationship inspired us to become more conscious stewards of our one and only home.

# Monks in Bunks

*"One doesn't thrive alone in autonomous isolation but,
rather, in relationship to others in shared social space."*
– JEREMY RIFKIN

Some of my favorite memories as a child revolve around the many
different people my parents would invite to stay with us for weeks
and sometimes months at a time. Diverse in every possible way,
they came from all over the globe. The guest list included actors and
archeologists, business people and artists, revolutionaries and tennis
champions, as well as students and holy men. Whether their visits were
motivated by business or pleasure, they were always a part of our
home, adding color and interest to our daily lives. I loved this extended
family with its divergent social interactions, varied viewpoints, interests,
and perspectives. The stories of our guests became windows through
which I could look out upon new worlds and ideas. It made life feel
both exciting and rich with possibility. In addition, my parents offered
an unwavering policy of inclusion. As their children, no matter what
disastrous mistake we might have made or what age we were, my
mother and father always had room for us in their home. This spirit of
generosity included our friends as well, many of whom lived with our
parents for extended periods of time whether or not we were even there.
Home was a place of welcome, regardless of an individual's situation.

Peter and I share this same love of including others in our home. We both enjoy having visitors stay with us. Something wonderful happens when we are joined in sharing our everyday life together; it creates community with whom we can learn, share, and celebrate. We are always happy to offer our home as a retreat, whether someone needs to grieve over a lost love, to begin a new project, or simply requires a place to stay.

To me, the idea that a couple can fulfill each other's social and relational needs is unfair and unrealistic. Peter is a wonderful husband, but he can't possibly take the place of my treasured women friends. I feel extremely fortunate that Devika, a poet and a teacher, has been our roommate for the past twenty years. It all began when she came to work at the Garden School. Because of the length of her commute, we invited her to spend Wednesday and Thursday evenings with us, returning to her home in Occidental at the end of the school week. During the two days she lives with us, she becomes part of our family. In the evening while making dinner, we find time to chat about what is going on in our lives, sharing our ideas, challenges, and stories. The extended time together means we can drop into real conversations and continue the thread of ideas into the next day or the next week. This intimate connection provides me with a type of companionship that is different from the sort that Peter and I share. Devika's presence in the house enriches our interactions and makes life more interesting. Having her as part of our extended family has been an ongoing pleasure.

I am certain that Peter values his male friends in much the same way. While I enjoy listening to their discussions, Peter's conversations with Uncle Doug about agro-ecological farming, wilderness conservation, or global economics and capitalism are ones I cannot duplicate. Nor could I carry on in the same way our friend Scott, a knowledgeable waterman, can on the topic of sailing canoes. This subject is something that he and Peter can discuss enthusiastically for hours at a time. Having these friendships has nourished our individual needs for companionship and supported our relationship to one another.

The same is surely true for the three of you. While Peter and I are always happy to engage with you on any subject, sometimes you might simply prefer to get Aunt Marci's advice or hear what Uncle Tim has to say. They have known all three of you since you were babies, and we have shared numerous adventures and holidays together. It makes complete sense that their perspectives are ones you value. Regardless of the subject, their views are founded in both a love for you and an intimate understanding of our family dynamics. Many other wonderful individuals compose this extended community of aunties and uncles (whether related or not). Each of them has offered you the opportunity to expand into diverse relationships with caring adults.

Some of our most treasured experiences have come through the vehicle of illness. Rick, who was thirty years old at the time, came to stay with us while going through numerous rounds of chemotherapy and radiation. He was a good friend and neighbor from our Esprit days in Germany, where he created, installed, and constantly updated the company's first computer system. He stopped to visit us, having just completed his lifelong dream of sailing through the Caribbean. When we met him at the airport, it was frighteningly clear. He was too sick to continue traveling. He moved into our home, and over the course of the next six months, made frequent trips to the hospital for treatments. In the end, these efforts couldn't stop the spread of cancer through his body. He died a week before Lake was born, and life felt inconceivably precious having lived through those last months with him.

Lance, twenty-eight, arrived at our home using a cane to get himself around. However, due to his combined illnesses of AIDS and ALS, he became a paraplegic within months, right in front of our eyes. His diagnosis was a death sentence he lived with every day, knowing he had less than a year to enjoy his life. Living with Lance, all of us, including the three of you, experienced the fragility of existence. We watched someone we loved transform from a healthy young man to an invalid in a wheelchair and finally to someone on his deathbed. Through it all, Lance modeled a positive relationship to suffering and death. Regardless of how difficult or painful his situation became, he maintained a courageous and accepting state of mind, accompanied by a genuine presence that could find humor in even the bleakest moments. I remember one summer morning seeing him at his favorite spot on our patio, his wheelchair rocked back against the picnic table. The sun was quite strong, and he was soaking in the warmth, a beer in one hand and a cigarette in the other. I waved to him and asked how he was doing.

"Great news!" he grinned. "There's no chance of me getting cancer!" He gave new meaning to the expression "die laughing," as his very funny jokes kept everyone around him smiling right up to the day he died.

For myself, sharing that year with Lance provided a sort of homeopathic remedy for the fear of dying. He allowed all of us to journey with him and digest a little of that fear each day. Taking care of him taught me the healing value of loving touch and inspired me to become certified as a massage therapist so I could practice hospice massage. Lance was a catalyst in my life, helping me to overcome my own fear of death and find a meaningful way to become involved in this process with others. Because of his presence, each of us was able to further cultivate a unique relationship to that mystery for which we are all destined.

One of the many blessings that emerged from the time spent with Lance is our relationship with Arthur. A master gardener and deeply wise and loving being, Arthur moved into what had been known as the Raven House (our second grade classroom) shortly after the school moved to its new location in downtown Mill Valley. He generously offered to help with the constant care Lance required. After Lance's death, Arthur continued to live with us, sharing both his extensive knowledge of plants along with his remarkable skills as a stonemason. We have all lived together for the last fifteen years, and we deeply value Arthur's powerful presence in our lives.

Some of our most memorable houseguests arrived on a summer day in 1998. We were in the process of remodeling our home on the mountain because our family bedroom was not going to accommodate your needs as adolescents. You were ages eight, nine, and ten. If we started right away, we could add a bedroom for each of you before you became teenagers. We decided to rent a house for the duration of the remodel so that we didn't have to live in a construction site.

A rental home in Stinson Beach had everything we needed—more, in fact. The house was L-shaped and built around a sunny courtyard, protected from the strong winds that define that region of the coast. One arm of the L consisted of a kitchen, living room, and a bedroom for Peter and me, while the other was composed of three small rooms complete with bunk beds.

We began envisioning how to wean the three of you from our family bedroom sleeping arrangement. Rather than force you to sleep alone in this new house, we decided to put three twin mattresses end to end, creating a giant day bed in the living room. Beside it, three large baskets held your comforters and pillows, which allowed the bed to double as a couch during the day. The transition turned out to be an easy one. At night, after a warm cup of tea, you fell asleep to the sounds of stories and of waves breaking upon the shore. Your clothes and treasured possessions were kept in the three little bedrooms that no one slept in.

We had been living in this home on the sand for about two weeks when the call came. A woman I had met briefly once before introduced herself and asked if we knew anyone who might be able to accommodate five Tibetan refugees who had just escaped from China. I told her I would call her back once I had a chance to speak with Peter. After a brief discussion, we decided to invite them to come and stay with us. How could we say no to this group of individuals whose needs were so real? After all, we had three bunk beds available. Monks in Bunks became the theme of our summer.

That was the beginning of our friendship with Arjia Rinpoche, Chunpay, Chen-li, Lousang, and Meido. Although they did not speak any English, they fit into our family life instantly with their innate understanding of how to live lightly and cooperatively with others. They stayed with us for the summer, taking English classes and joining in with our daily activities. They enriched our lives in many unexpected ways. Every morning and evening our house was filled with the chanting of Tibetan prayers. Delicious smells wafted from the kitchen as Lousang made traditional dishes of homemade noodles and momos. They were each so helpful that life was actually easier with them in our home. Eventually they all integrated themselves into American life while still maintaining a vibrant and supportive relationship to their own culture. Our friendship has continued to remain strong over the years.

Moving back to our mountain home a year and a half later, I wondered how you would adjust to sleeping in your own bedrooms for the first time. Each one of you ran excitedly to your new room and proceeded to move in. Peter and I walked into our freshly painted bedroom, now futon-free and with only our bed against the wall. We paused, amazed at the transition that had just taken place. Taking stock of my emotions in that moment, I realized I felt absolutely complete, with no sadness or regret.

I thought to myself that perhaps this is what all of life's transitions could be like. If you do something as well as you can and with all of your heart, when the time comes for it to end, rather than feeling regret, you feel a sense of completeness and peace. I am still testing this theory, but so far, so good.

With your departure for college and the arrival of our empty nest era, we found that because we have an extended family who enjoy coming to stay with us, the house has rarely felt sad or empty. The joy of sharing every day together has been replaced with the pleasure of watching you design your own lives as young adults. We delight in those times when you return and are always happy to include your friends as part of our family. The large transitions in life are easier to bear when surrounded by a circle of people you love. We are most grateful for their company.

# Putting out Fires

*"Mistakes are wonderful opportunities to learn."*
– JANE NELSON

Although we were unaware of it at the time, your teenage years were foreshadowed one rainy, winter afternoon when you were ages three, four, and five. Peter was away on a trip, and I was in the kitchen with the three of you, crayons and paints spread out on the small table along with a bowl full of cookie dough made from your grandmother Peggie's favorite recipe. I was unknowingly about to make a really bad decision.

As often happens to mothers of young children, I had contracted a winter cold that wouldn't let go, and it was beginning to move down into my lungs. When the pharmacy called that afternoon to let me know my prescription was ready, I found myself in the midst of a dilemma. It was Saturday, and if I didn't go to town and pick it up, I would have to wait until Monday, as the pharmacy was closed on Sundays. Peter had taken the van, leaving only the tiny, red sports car that had no back seat and definitely no room for the three of you. Prone to pneumonia, I was pretty sure my infection was going to get worse if I waited. What should I do? It was late in the afternoon, the pharmacy didn't deliver, and I needed to go before their doors closed. Could I leave you by yourselves for the twenty minutes it would take for me to collect the prescription? My mind, muddled by illness, saw it as the only choice. I gathered you together and explained the situation, emphasizing the need for safety and assuring you I would return as quickly as possible to bake the cookies. You all seemed to comprehend the situation, so I threw on my rain jacket and bolted out the door.

Twenty minutes later I returned. Opening the door, I was met with the intoxicating smell of chocolate cookies baking in the oven. The teakettle was whistling, and I heard the sound of someone chopping wood in the living room. The table was set for a tea party, with neatly arranged cups and plates for four. As I turned the corner I saw Woods, a small red ax in his hands, poised to chop a piece of kindling in half that Lake was holding steady. Sitting right next to them was Coleman, diligently building a fire on the wooden floor about two feet in front of the actual fireplace.

"Welcome home Momma! We're making a cozy party for you!"

I had to admire your achievements, all born out of an impulse to take care of your sick mom. You had managed to accomplish, without an accident, a number of potentially dangerous projects that included scalding hot water, a newly sharpened ax, and an open fire. The fact that the house could have burnt down, well, that was just an error in judgment—mainly my own! I helped you to move the fire off the floor and into the fireplace just as the well-placed kindling ignited into a healthy blaze. Little did I know at the time that the theme of near accidents and parties had just begun.

Years passed and Peter and I found ourselves in a home with three teenagers. This was both a challenging and deeply rewarding time. We knew we needed to allow you your freedom. Supporting you in the ways we could, relying on positive discipline to help us communicate with one another, and allowing you to make your own individual choices felt like the natural next step. Paradoxically, this letting go style of parenting allowed us to maintain the close relationships we had always shared with each of you. To understand why we chose this approach, I need to explain how my parents raised me. In my childhood home there was no such thing as punishment. I don't ever remember my parents saying "No." When a problem arose, they would help me to consider it by asking questions, letting me express my perception of the event, and then sharing their perspectives. They would reflect the situation back to me and describe what they could imagine as the consequences or benefits of different actions. How I decided to solve an issue was my choice. Knowing they were on my side, I was eager to hear their opinions. Their kindness and understanding allowed me to keep my dignity intact.

Making my own decisions from an early age was both sobering and empowering. This doesn't mean I always made the wise choice or did what my parents suggested. Often it was in making the wrong one that I learned the most. Natural consequences can be a powerful teacher and don't need additional punishments to make their point. Rather than complying with my parents' wishes out of fear, I learned to trust my own intuition and look for successful solutions to my problems. Their gift to me was one of self-reliance.

Peter and I chose to raise you in that same style. There would be no such thing as punishment in our family, knowing your desire not to disappoint us was a more powerful incentive than any restrictive measure could be. We never grounded you, set curfews, or restricted anything other than the amount of time you spent in front of a television screen, video game, or computer. We wanted home to be the place where you could come with both your successes and your problems, knowing we were there to help consider options and solutions if you wanted our opinions. Having had your needs met, you wanted to meet ours. This may sound utopian, but we actually found it to be the case. It didn't mean there weren't disagreements or frustrating exchanges. If conversations began to become hurtful or divisive, we would take a break. No one can communicate well when angry, including parents. We knew if we each regained our calm and considered a problem together, solutions could be found that would work for everyone.

We intentionally made our home a place where all of your friends would feel comfortable to come and hang out, both so we knew you were safe and so we could be a part of your life while still allowing you to maintain the natural privacy adolescents require. Often, with our permission, you would invite your classmates to come and enjoy a party at our house. Our request was that they all bring sleeping bags and spend the night. The only thing we asked during these lively gatherings was that our home be respected. We would start the party with dinner. There was something about orienting everyone with a homemade meal at the beginning of the evening that personalized the experience, and no one ever took advantage of what we offered. In the morning, Peter would make a waffle breakfast. By welcoming your friends into our lives, we were able to get to know them as well as watch them grow up. This helped us to feel connected to your world, and we still enjoy their company.

When you became sexually active, we welcomed your boyfriends and girlfriends into our home, allowing them to spend the night with you and join us for breakfast in the morning. We wanted to normalize the experience of a relationship and all that comes along with it, and of course we always preferred having you at home with us. When your plans took you to other places, our one requirement was that you let us know where you were so we wouldn't worry. We also made it clear that you could always call us at any hour to come and get you if a situation arose where you couldn't make it home on your own. Our only rule, in essence, was, "Be kind to yourselves and be kind to others."

Over the years, each of you has had your fair share of ups and downs, with plenty of fires that needed to be put out. There have been car accidents, speeding tickets, broken bones, and broken hearts. But even in the midst of these complications, you have taken responsibility, included us in a respectful way, listened to our advice, and solved the problem at hand. Our response remains the same: you are capable and trusted. So when a situation has gone up in flames, you have usually been able to douse it on your own, knowing that our help was there if you needed it. Home is a safe place to bring both joys and problems, and (knock on wood) it hasn't burned down yet.

# PART THREE

# CROSSROADS

# Coming Out of the Closet

*"Since we don't know where we're going,*
*we have to stick together in case somebody gets there."*
– KEN KESEY

M r. Thomas was not your typical fifth grade teacher. It wasn't just the colorful bow ties he sported or the longish hair that spilled over the collar of his pressed white shirt and worn tweed jacket. His gentle manner and kindly presence could be counted on, yet the twinkle in his eyes revealed a delightfully rebellious spirit, clearly affiliated with the counterculture of the sixties. It set him apart from the other teachers at the small day school in Pasadena that I attended, and we all loved him for it. As ten-year-olds, we stood balanced on the summit of our childhood while the beckoning lands of adolescence stretched out before us. Mr. Thomas was a guide in whom we had complete trust. We were happy to follow him into this new territory.

"Today we are going to do something a little bit different," he said, turning off all the lights in the classroom. Reaching into his tattered leather briefcase, he removed three white candles and placed them neatly on the table in front of the center blackboard, the one with the roll-up map attached to it. Opening one of the drawers of his brown desk, he pulled out a colorful box and a lighter. The box contained long, thin sticks that he proceeded to ignite along with the candles. He blew on the sticks and the small flame was replaced with a thin string of smoke that perfumed the unusually still classroom. We were spellbound. None of us had ever imagined such a thing could happen in our own homeroom. He was breaking all of the rules, and we were thrilled.

He pulled down the world map, and instead of seeing the expected seven continents, we sat face to face with a symbol none of us had ever seen before: a three-foot diameter circle with what looked like an ornately drawn symbol for the number three in its center. "Everyone please take off your shoes and sit on top of your desks, like this." Placing polished loafers neatly beside his large wooden chair, Mr. Thomas leapt up and landed gracefully in a cross-legged position. Too stunned to even question this request, we all climbed onto our desks and tried our best to copy him.

"Close your eyes gently. Take a nice, deep breath. Breathe in; breathe out. Let's do this together three times. Relax and let all of your concerns melt away. Notice how it feels. Notice how you feel. Quiet your mind and let your thoughts settle. Stillness allows us to rest in our true selves: that place where we feel absolutely at home. Take another deep breath. Enjoy the present moment." Wanting to make sure I wasn't the only one following his instructions, I opened my eyes to take a peek at my classmates. To my relief, they were all doing their best to sit quietly and follow along. I closed my eyes once again.

"The image on the wall is the Sanskrit symbol for OM. OM stands for our complete interconnectedness with all of life. It is only in our minds that any separation exists. Our true nature is one with all of existence. Remember this. Feel your seamless connection to one another, to the earth, and to the universe. The purest expression of this connection is love. Love is the greatest gift we can give. Love is the path to self-awareness. Remember this moment. Enjoy the stillness." We took a few more breaths together, after which he recommended that we open our eyes and return to our seats without speaking. He then moved to the classroom record player and put on the Beatles song, "All You Need Is Love."

I don't know what kind of long-term effect this experience had on my classmates, but I know for certain this was a pivotal moment for me, leaving a lasting impression that would define the journey of my life. Since that morning in Mr. Thomas's classroom, I became spiritually curious. Instead of going to college after high school, I traveled to India, where I lived on an ashram devoted to the teachings of Meher Baba, a spiritual teacher who had died several years prior to my visit. While his remaining disciples were welcoming and told wonderful stories, it wasn't the same as being in the presence of a living master. At the ashram, I experienced only glimpses of the oneness that so many spoke of. After several months I was left hungry for something more, but I didn't know how to find it. I returned home, still a seeker, and earned my undergraduate degrees in Religious Studies and Studio Art. Graduating from college and needing a job, I found myself in the world of design, which required all of my attention for the next ten years.

When Peter and I returned to California, a new chapter in my life began. After seven years of living in Europe, moving to Mill Valley felt like coming home. I was so happy to once again be part of a community that didn't feel foreign, whose values I understood and shared. In Marin, as in most of Northern California, the pursuit of consciousness was an accepted and valued endeavor. Meditation retreats of all kinds were offered as well as a huge variety of classes and seminars on just about everything. It felt great to once again be in a place where spiritual curiosity was encouraged and fostered.

The same yearning that took me to India in my teenage years called to me once again. I wanted to cultivate an understanding of the questions that lived in my heart: Who am I? What am I doing here? I knew there was something I needed to know, but I wasn't sure exactly what it was. Because of these questions, I became interested in the various schools of Buddhism and the meditation practices associated with them. I attended many retreats with inspiring teachers, all of which were very beneficial and helped me to recognize the nature of mind and the tendencies it has to create suffering. This by itself was a very valuable gift.

However, even with all of these opportunities, inside I was still longing for something—something deeper.

My dream was that one day I might spend time with a living guru who could help me discover what I was looking for. In his book, *Be Love Now: The Path of the Heart*, Ram Dass, one of my favorite spiritual teachers, describes the importance of a guru this way:

> If you think of the spiritual path as the road home to your true Self, a teacher is someone standing next to you, pointing and giving directions, while the guru is up the road ahead, beckoning to you from your destination. He or she is someone who has already made the journey and knows the lay of the land. In fact, the guru knows it's all One, that the journey is an illusion and that it's all right here, and that your being is just another face of the One. The guru's job is to get you to know that too.

The way a guru helps you to know yourself is through a direct transmission of this understanding. The guru becomes a model of total awareness. In his or her presence, when we pay attention, a glimpse of everything as One becomes possible.

When you were ages seven, eight, and nine, I had the chance to meet a true guru. Poonja-ji lived in Lucknow, a semi-industrial city in India known for its beautifully embroidered kurtas, traditional long-sleeved cotton shirts. People whom I trusted vouched for Poonja-ji's authenticity as a guru. He was a teacher from the Advaita tradition, which views non-dual consciousness as our natural state. Advaita means non-dual or not two. Its basic premise is that everything is interconnected, and we have the opportunity to experience this as our true, innate identity.

Poonja-ji taught that self-realization, or the realization of the oneness of who we are, is not some distant goal only a few can attain. Advaita teachings tell us that our experience of belonging is already here and is, in fact, who we are—that oneness is the fundamental quality of everything. Our natural state is one of non-dual consciousness. We are not separate from any one or any thing. I yearned for that experience. This was my opportunity to sit in the presence of an enlightened being. I knew I needed to go. Peter was very generous, offering to take best care of you while I was gone. Even so, I didn't want to be away from you for long, and I needed to make this trip brief. I organized one that was seven days from start to finish. If this living guru/transmission business wasn't true for me, at least I would know it.

Downtown Lucknow isn't exactly a tourist destination. As I looked out of my hotel window at the busy streets teeming with life, a film of diesel exhaust seemed to cover everything, including the people. Poonja-ji's house was a twenty-minute cab drive from the city center, assuming there wasn't a cow in the road. The neighborhood he lived in was a quiet one. Cinderblock buildings painted bright colors bordered the dirt road where I was dropped off, having been invited to lunch with him and a few other devotees in his home.

It could not have been a more modest house or a more simple lunch. I was struck by how gracious he was toward all of us, inquiring as to how our flights had been and how we were feeling after all of the travel. I don't know what I had expected, but I felt like I was having lunch with my grandmother. A part of me thought: I just traveled more than halfway around the world for this? I had purchased some lovely kurtas, but that wasn't really my reason for coming.

The next morning we assembled at a small gathering hall close to his home. There were about fifty followers already packed into the hall, everyone sitting cross-legged on the floor, quietly awaiting him. He arrived shortly after we had settled ourselves, and sitting on a small stage, he began his teaching, known as satsang.

He was a brilliant man, and his stories had a depth and humor that made them both engaging and compelling. There was a lot to learn just by listening to him. After these talks, he would open up for questions from the audience, occasionally inviting the person asking the question to come sit with him on the stage. He was attentive and genuine in his responses, answering questions in a way that felt personal and extremely appropriate for each individual. Some people were clearly moved by their experiences with him, but I was uncertain about exactly what they had felt.

The few days I had the opportunity to attend satsang passed quickly. On my final day, I had pretty much given up on the idea of something out of the ordinary happening. It had all been a good experience but nothing exceptional from my perspective. His dharma talk was wrapping up. As usual, he invited comments from the audience. Something he said had triggered a question within me, so I raised my hand.

Before I knew what was happening, I was sitting on the small stage across from him, his dark eyes holding mine with an unblinking gaze. I can't remember what was said, but I will never forget what I became. Falling into his presence, I was surrounded by a vastness unlike anything I had ever known. Like a fish swept up in a river that was boundless, I belonged fully to the experience. I wasn't just surrounded by it; I was it. I was no longer in the limited self, known as Mimi, but instead became the life force itself, existing beyond any kind of personal identity. My being was thoroughly connected with no sense of separation or longing. It wasn't at all frightening. A harmonious inclusivity colored the entire experience, and I felt embraced. I was at home with my true self, a completely undivided experience of oneness. Finally his gaze released me, and I surfaced.

Stumbling back to my seat, I realized where I was and tried to piece my identity as Mimi together. It was difficult. I really didn't want to leave the reality I had just experienced—that place of perfect oneness. I wasn't sure if I would ever be the same again. Fortunately, as it turned out, I wouldn't. The lesson from Poonja-ji became a touchstone in my life. I experienced the awareness of complete belonging without separation. I found I was able to return to it by quieting my mind and resting in stillness.

Two days later, Peter met me at the airport. "How was it?" he asked. I tried to explain the entire experience on the drive home, but even I wasn't sure what had just happened. It was wonderful to walk in the door of our house and be met by all of you, full of hugs and kisses.

But returning to the everyday busyness of family after a direct transmission from a guru was at best an abrupt transition.

That's how I found myself escaping into the serenity of our walk-in closet. I needed a quiet moment to myself. I sat on the floor next to a huge pile of laundry that begged for attention, while your voices called to me from downstairs. How could I combine the experience of the last week with being a mother? Was there a way of integrating inner stillness and conscious connection while living in this bustling reality? Should I renounce everything and go live in a cave? How could I possibly leave my family? I couldn't. This was going to require a balanced approach that included everything and excluded nothing.

Thankfully, in that moment, I remembered that many others before me had faced the conundrum of how to combine daily life with a reflective practice. The Hindu religion answers the question by recognizing four main chapters of life, beginning with the Student, followed by the Householder, then the Retired Person, and finally the Ascetic or Monk. Each stage allows for the combination of day-to-day activities with one's spiritual practice. I was a Householder. Family, home, and work provided endless opportunities for me to remember what Poonja-ji had shown me. Everything I did, beginning with the smallest task, could be performed with the intention of cultivating loving kindness. By imbuing my actions with this awareness, those around me might experience a natural sense of belonging, of being at home. This realization was a timely gift. It brought with it a sense of completeness—I no longer needed to search for meaning; I was right in the middle of it. I didn't need to leave behind everyday life but rather engage with it as fully as possible. Choosing to view my life in this way has made even the most mundane tasks more interesting. I don't always do as well with it as I wish I did, but it gives me something to shoot for—I try my best to reflect connection.

Knowing that I could integrate everything I loved so dearly came as a tremendous relief. I felt thoroughly complete, no longer looking for that missing piece in my life. Home at last, I opened the closet door and went downstairs to make dinner.

# Going Home

*"Tell me, what is it you plan to do*
*with your one wild and precious life?"*

– "THE SUMMER DAY"
by MARY OLIVER

Ends offer beginnings. But it doesn't always feel that way when it's happening to you. Our home can offer a valuable familiarity when we are entering into a difficult and unknown realm. This was the experience I had when we decided to bring Coco, your grandfather, home to die.

My parents, after living for more than sixty-five years in Pasadena, were moving to a senior community in Palo Alto. It was a place where they could be closer to their children and grandchildren, free from the responsibilities of caring for a house. As their children, we arranged a Hawaiian honeymoon for them while we moved all of their belongings into the spacious, brand-new apartment. The large windows offered a postcard view of the setting sun as it dropped behind the mountains, giving the high-ceilinged walls a warm glow.

Your aunt Janie and I had just finished hanging the last of the paintings when the phone rang. It was our mother, explaining that Coco had been admitted to the ICU in Kona. The doctors had not been able to diagnose his illness, and his vital signs were rapidly going downhill. Coco's one request was that he be brought back to California to die.

My brother Lindley, upon hearing the news, volunteered to fly over immediately and retrieve our parents.

We met them at the airport the following evening, and it was clear my father was failing. Coco, even as he sat in a wheelchair, wore his signature three-piece suit with silken tie and fluffed hankie. Maintaining his composure and bombproof dignity, he insisted on going back to their new place for the night instead of heading straight to the Stanford Hospital. We agreed, happy at the thought of keeping him with us.

After our arrival, we rolled him from one room to another so he could see the entirety of the new apartment. His spirits seemed to lift as he nodded in approval at the placement of familiar furnishings and family heirlooms. Each piece welcomed him back—keepers of treasured memories. By the next morning his pain had become unmanageable, and he was admitted to the hospital. Two days and countless tests later, we all realized nothing more could be done. It was time to bring him home.

Instead of putting his hospital bed in one of the two large bedrooms, we decided the best place for him would be in the living room where he could feel our presence continually. We placed the bed close to the fireplace, next to the French doors that opened onto a small, sunny balcony. His view was of the living and dining area, so when we sat down for meals it felt like he was joining us, taking his usual place at the head of the table.

He lasted for four days, swimming in between consciousness and morphine-clouded dreams. The tank of oxygen hummed beside him as an ever-present gathering of family fielded phone calls, read the daily finance section in the Wall Street Journal to him, told jokes, and reminisced while looking at the photo albums your grandmother had created over the years.

I found comfort in cooking. The kitchen was a place where I could rest in the middle of things. The white counters were crowded with wooden bowls full of purple onions, spring garlic, tangelos, and Meyer lemons. Fresh parsley, cilantro, and dill waited by the worn cutting board, while cornbread cooled on the counter next to a pot of steaming black bean soup. We enveloped my father with all of his favorite smells. His appetite had disappeared days before, so we fed him with the aromas. Because of his lifetime love affair with chocolate, we baked brownies and chocolate chip cookies, filling the entire house with their delicious fragrance. Occasionally we would brush the insides of his lips with a dab of the batter, hoping to sweeten the moment, or better yet, to lure him back.

But even chocolate failed to stall the inevitable. On the fourth and final day, Granny, drained by the long hours and the brokenness of my father, her lover and partner of more than sixty-five years, retired to her bedroom for an afternoon nap. Pulling a chocolate cake out of the oven, I heard the rhythmic rasping of my father's breathing change. It was lighter, with long pauses in between the guttural inhale and the whispered exhale. I stepped around the corner to glance at him and knew at once we were in the final stretch. We woke my mother, and everyone gathered around his bed, often trading places so that we might all have a chance to hold his hand and express our love. Granny, her arms wrapped around Coco, lightly showered him with kisses. His breathing shifted. Your cousin Alex, then one year old, was busy exploring the world underneath Coco's bed—life and death braiding into one. Another breath and the gurgling sound in his lungs disappeared. A radiance touched his face during his final inhalation, and the next moment he was gone.

I had heard the word "keening" before. It is defined as a lamentation for the dead uttered in a loud wailing voice or sometimes a wordless cry. It is a word I knew but had never experienced until that moment when my mother began. Wailing words of love, a focused river of grief flooded the room, drawing us all along in its torrential currents. Her sorrowful keening was like a raft, almost able to carry her across the abyss that now separated them. I can't say how long that lasted. Her cries finally dissolved into stillness, leaving her emptied. Standing on the threshold between life and death, she was unable to accompany him any further. He had disappeared into a realm just out of her grasp, and she was left on the shore with the rest of us.

We all looked at one another. Stillness filled the room as sunset dressed the home in golden tones. Coco had passed over, leaving us in a disarray of both relief and sorrow. We held hands, forming a circle around him, each of us offering up unrehearsed words of love to our father, husband, and grandfather.

Coco, a recovered alcoholic, used to joke that he had been a member of Alcoholics Anonymous for fifteen years, ten of them sober. Recovery had been a difficult road, but he emerged from the journey a wiser and kinder man. We had saved the champagne for just this moment. "It's been long enough!" My mother dipped her finger into the rosy bubbles that now matched the color of the walls and wiped Coco's lips. "You deserve a drink!" she laughed, while tears streamed from her eyes. We all raised our glasses. "We love you, Coco. We love you." It was May 18th, 2006. He had lived for eighty-seven vibrant years.

During my time working at the Zen Hospice in San Francisco, I learned the value of staying with the body after death. At the hospice, caregivers and families would take time to wash the deceased (often with warm jasmine tea) and dress them in their favorite clothes or wrap them in a shroud of beautiful fabric. Immediately after the death, all of the medical supplies were removed from the room and replaced with fresh flowers, candles, and pictures of the departed. Importance was placed on spending time with the body, allowing everyone to come and sit, say goodbye, and experience both the finality and the calm.

So this is what we did with Coco. According to county law, we were allowed to keep his body at home for forty-eight hours after the time of death. We cleared the room of all the medications, the oxygen tank, and the wheelchair. Cleaning him with warm water and washcloths, we then wrapped his body in an ivory-colored raw silk curtain that my niece, Aya, and I purchased an hour after his death at the shopping center across the street.

"Only one?" the salesgirl had inquired.

"Yes, please," we answered.

"Would you like the hardware to go with it?"

"No, thank you," we replied, "but does it come in an extra long?" Coco was a tall man, and we needed the additional yardage. Fortunately, it did come in his size. Returning home, we wrapped him in the silk and placed his head on an embroidered blue and white pillow. As a final touch, we arranged gardenias (his favorite flower) on the bed. A stickler for every detail, Coco was a dashing dresser and put a high premium on looking good. We all agreed that he would have approved of his appearance, considering the circumstances.

We sat down to dinner a few hours later. Candles were lit and Coco's favorite recording of Cole Porter songs played softly, accompanying our stories and memories of times past. For dessert we had chocolate cake, Coco's favorite.

That evening I stayed with my mother. In the middle of the night we found ourselves sitting on the couch across from Coco's body, trying to imagine how to proceed. New to this community, my mother felt unable to organize a large memorial service. Where would we even do it? The next morning, my sister Janie arrived early, and we continued the discussion over breakfast. "I can't imagine Coco would want to have a church service," my mother said. "After all, he never even went to church." My sister looked at my mother, then turned around to look at my father, deceased in the living room.

"You know what Coco would say about a church service?" We looked at her for the answer. "He would say, 'Not over my dead body!'" The timing was perfect; it felt great to laugh at such a good joke. And we knew for certain Coco would have loved it.

The day unfolded with family and friends coming and going. Saying goodbye to someone when he is dying is a very difficult thing to do. Having the body at home allowed everyone the opportunity to sit with him one last time and say those final words, somehow easier to say when faced with the finality of death. It is something like the experience of cutting a flower. Once snipped from the stalk, it is no longer alive, yet it still appears to contain some sort of life force that then ebbs away slowly. There comes a point with the body, sometimes immediately upon death and sometimes much later, when that life force has clearly departed. Like an empty shell on the beach, the body remains only a vessel for the life that once inhabited it. Experiencing firsthand this sense of complete departure can help us to accept that our loved one has gone.

Day two of our vigil with Coco was a quiet one. We knew he would be cremated that evening, and most of our family had already said their goodbyes and departed. My mother was napping, and the apartment was quiet. I sat in the warm stillness of the filtered sun next to Coco. I relished this place of rest—a trough of calm in between my unbidden waves of grief. In that moment, I unexpectedly felt something land on my chest, and a flow of warmth surrounded my heart. It was coming directly from my father—his essence entering my physical body—a transfusion of pure energy. Was it just my imagination that saw a flash of golden light move between us? Whatever it was, the essence of Coco entered my heart and has been there ever since. Always a part of me, I draw on it whenever I miss him. I cannot explain this phenomenon, but I am grateful for it. If we had not chosen to keep him with us after his death, that moment would have been lost. Bringing our father home to die instilled the apartment with his presence, creating a soothing connection to him. An indelible memory of Coco accompanied my mother as she began to settle into her new life.

We were all unsure how Granny would fare without Coco. She was in a natural state of shock, having lost her lifelong partner. We watched as she slowly found her footing in the new territory of Palo Alto. New friends, new home, new neighborhood—everything required her full engagement and took time to cultivate. We were all deeply moved by her ability to recreate a full and meaningful life. Her courage and determination allowed her to begin again. During this time, Coco's ashes sat on her mantle, keeping her company as she rebuilt her reality. She was certain she would know when she could part with them, and she did.

It was two years later when we celebrated Coco's memorial service on the banks of the Merced River. Every May my parents embarked on a road trip to Yosemite, where they would celebrate my mother's birthday. Springtime in that valley is stunning. Lilacs and dogwoods blossom in the green meadows while above them waterfalls grace the soaring granite walls. During these annual visits, my parents enjoyed taking their favorite walks, always bringing a picnic to share beside the Merced River.

"We are going to have Coco's memorial in Yosemite. That was his church." My mother had decided, and we were all happy to make it happen. We wanted to include as many family members as possible. Fortunately we were in no hurry and had a year to organize tents and cabins for everyone.

On the morning of my mother's birthday, May 8th, 2008, we gathered as a family next to the Merced. Sitting in a circle under the pines, we shared Coco stories and played his favorite songs. We ate chocolate and told the jokes we had learned from him. The punch lines felt like old friends, still making us laugh even after all this time. After our circle, we carried the polished wooden box containing his ashes to the small stone bridge and released them into the river with handfuls of gardenias. The ashes and flowers formed a white cloud in the sparkling water as it danced away to the sea. Coco was free.

Every year on my mother's birthday we revisit the bridge and bring a basket of roses from our garden. With each flower we toss into the river, we tell a story of Coco. The grandeur of the valley reminds us of him and soothes us with a reflection of his memory. Remembering him by the river has become a family ritual that keeps him close to our hearts.

# The Secret Ingredient

*"I still think that one of the pleasantest of all emotions
is to know that I, I with my brain and hands,
have nourished my beloved few, that I have concocted a stew
or a story, a rarity or a plain dish, to sustain them
truly against the hungers of the world."*

– MFK FISHER

Made with love. A common enough expression, but what does it mean, exactly? I was considering this while making a pie with my very favorite baking pumpkin, the Winter Luxury. Where was the love in this pie? Was it tucked in the fat seeds, the ones I picked out of the gooey orange threads while thinking about where to plant them next spring? Or was it in the ginger cookie crust I pressed into my favorite extra-large, red pie dish? Perhaps it was in our hens' eggs and their sunny yolks that mixed into a perfect pale yellow with the cream's white thickness. Maybe it lurked in the sweet smell of nutmeg, freshly ground from a big brown seed. The scents of ginger, vanilla, and clove might be its source, or was it the warmth of the stove wafting the sweet and savory pumpkin aroma throughout our home on that cloudy winter day? It would have been easy to believe the pie absorbed all of these things and the joy I felt in knowing all three of you were coming home. Maybe it did. We would soon be sharing a few precious days together. Time with the three of you was rare, now that you had all gone off to college.

Our empty nest, though anticipated, still came as a shock. It was late August, 2009, when Lake left for school. The unusual quiet in our home that first evening marked her departure. I sat on her bedroom floor immersed in the grief of knowing the last of you children had left home. As I looked around her room, a turquoise nest holding all of her left-behind treasures, I felt like one of them. I knew the chapter we had enjoyed as a family for the last twenty-two years was now complete. The identity I had assumed, one that revolved around the daily tasks of parenting, community activities, and school boards was also at an end. In that moment, it seemed I had not only lost my job, I had lost all of you as well.

Although I had heard other parents, especially mothers, speak of the difficult transition that occurred when their last child left home, I hadn't anticipated that coming to terms with it would be such a very real challenge. For over two decades I had poured all of my creativity, energy, and attention into our life as a family. Suddenly that role was gone. I recognized that not only were my children getting older, but so was I.

It was during this vulnerable period that I was invited to a party composed mostly of people in their thirties. For the first time, I had the shocking experience of feeling invisible. I came home and found myself looking in the mirror, wondering about the sanity of a facelift. How should one grow old in a culture that so values youth? Aging is a reminder that we won't be here forever, that life is short. Acceptance, even appreciation of all the oncoming changes felt like the best approach. It was time to embrace the bitter sweetness of impermanence.

Parenting never ends; it just transforms itself. Over the months that followed my night of despair in Lake's room, I realized our roles as parents were as needed as ever, just in different ways. The empty nest becomes full once again as you return, only now with partners and friends that you love. It has been a pleasure watching you blossom into adults. As for aging, no face lift can protect me from the inevitable. I have decided to enjoy my smile lines and silver hair, this body that has given birth to three children and has seen me through almost sixty years of life, and the wisdom that comes from it all.

The passing beauty of life and all we cherish offers us the opportunity to notice it, now. Living into life fully and treasuring all we can is the appropriate response to the inevitability of change. My best advice is that you fall in love with life. Cultivate a full relationship with all things that call to you, make you curious, and bring you joy. Passionate engagement is both the secret and the sacred ingredient for each of us.

That day in the kitchen with all of you home for the holidays, I fell in love with the pie and everything about it. The blessing of an orange pumpkin filled my afternoon. It became a timepiece, marking the season, the orbit of our planet, this chapter in my life. An expression of the soil, its ingredients included long summer days, a waxing and waning moon amidst starry skies, the sounds of the summer creek as it flowed past our garden. We had nourished this pumpkin and it would nourish us. It seemed quite impossible to tell where we ended and it began. Into the bowl I scraped the delicate yellow from its tough shell, easily adding into it all of my love for you. Once the pie had baked and cooled, we gathered as a family to share the thick slices—celebrating the moment together, tasting all of life in each bite.

# A Knock on the Door

*"It's not living in perpetual harmony that produces pleasure.*
*If that were so, we'd be happy living on the beach all of our lives.*
*It's the moment when some tension is erased. So a happy life*
*has its recurring set of rhythms: difficulty to harmony,*
*difficulty to harmony. And it is all propelled by the desire*
*for that moment when the inner and outer patterns mesh."*

– DAVID BROOKS

I heard the knock on the door. Actually, it wasn't the first time she had come back for a visit. We had kept in touch since that fateful day in Düsseldorf when, realizing she didn't have my full attention, my pre-motherhood self flitted out the door. As much as I wanted her to stay, I knew she had made the right decision. It simply didn't feel possible to meet your needs and still manifest her dreams and visions. We (she and I) didn't have a lengthy conversation about it. I unknowingly had already chosen my path when Peter and I decided to have a family. I just didn't know it at the time.

I opened the door and welcomed her in. I knew I needed to rediscover myself—to dig deep and find the things in life that meant something to me, that called to me, that inspired me. I didn't want to fill up my life in order to avoid this new emptiness. I needed to let myself germinate just like the peas we planted when you were young. Wanting to be close friends again, I entered into a personal inquiry: Who was I before family? What did I love? Was I still that person? What do I love now? I found myself talking to the huge redwood that lives in our garden, asking for guidance or at the very least a small hint as to what I should do with the rest of my life. Redwoods are slow to answer, but they are very reliable. The clear response was delivered through its stable and rooted presence. Sit still and listen.

This ongoing journey is complete with the highs and lows inherent in the very personal nature of the creative process. I keep a favorite childhood photograph of myself nearby, reminding me of where I began and the continuum of spirit that propels me.

# The Evolution of a Marriage

*"May you know love as an adventure,*
*where each step and every stumble*
*bring you closer to the truth of another's soul,*
*and thus, closer to your own."*

– MARC IAN BARASCH

For ten dollars I became a minister. It was an honor to be asked by Marci and Jib if I would preside over their wedding ceremony. In order to have a valid signature on their marriage certificate, Marci purchased a membership for me in the Universal Life Church, which was offering very reasonable rates to anyone who wanted to become a minister. The credo of the church, "We are all children of the same universe," sounded quite agreeable. The fact that becoming a minister was free (the ten dollars was a contribution to the church from Marci) and required nothing from the newly ordained was also appealing. This was my kind of church.

Over the years, I have had the pleasure of performing weddings for other friends as well. Doing so has allowed me the opportunity to reflect on what makes a happy partnership. As newlyweds, it is nearly impossible to fully understand the depth of the commitment we have made to one another. The notion of the rest of your life is somewhat unfathomable, and the idea of partnering with another person for that duration even more so. It takes a leap of faith to venture into this mutual decision, but there are a few things of which you can be sure. The love you have for one another will go through many incarnations, and you will have the chance to reinvent it over and over. A happy marriage will have moments of unhappiness. If you pick someone whom you like as much as you love, someone you can accept just as he or she is, these complicated passages will be easier.

Growing up together as a couple requires cultivating both the ability to communicate and the humility to listen. It's not about winning or losing an argument. Rather the intent is to come out on the other side together, with a greater understanding of the other person's needs and your love for one another intact. Our friend, Jane Bryan Jones, a marriage and family therapist, offers her suggestions for keeping a marriage vibrant. At the top of her list is, "If you don't want to talk about it, talk about it!" Over the past twenty-five years, Peter and I have found this to be absolutely true. In fact, as difficult as an issue might be to discuss, we have found that expressing our feelings honestly (with kindness and a willingness to listen) is both scary and exciting. It opens up previously unexplored terrain for a marriage and allows new growth and consideration of old patterns. It requires skillful communication and clarity.

One of the crucial components for a positive exchange of feelings is timing. Jane also says, "A bottle of wine and a tough conversation are a deadly combination." The time for these conversations is not when you are tired, busy, intoxicated, driving, angry, about to go see friends, or when the children are around. Find a spacious moment with a window of time around it. If these are hard to come by, make an appointment with one another. Whatever you do, don't stuff it under the rug. Resentment will burn a hole in your heart, and the radiance of your love will diminish, leaving the marriage dull and lifeless.

Learn how to see the humor in your own behavior. Our patterns rarely change. Peter and I have had arguments about this or that ever since we first met. After all this time together, the flow of these conversations is fairly predictable. We wade through our concerns, get upset, make compromises, and try our best to find some common ground. We have learned not to compare our efforts, trusting instead in the certainty that we are each doing our best. We remember not to say *never* or *always* when describing each other's perceived shortcomings and our responses to them. We usually conduct ourselves with kindness, giving one another the benefit of the doubt. We are, after all, on the same team. Coming out on the other side, we shake off negative emotions as quickly as possible. This takes a lot of self-discipline. A part of me would much prefer to sulk and feel righteous, but I know that isn't the best approach. The relief comes in being able to finish the discussion and move on, but even this requires some work. Take some deep breaths and calm down. If you make an effort to let go of the tension, after about twenty minutes your brain will move out of fight or flight and allow the residue of conflict to dissolve.

Peter and I continue to imagine and deepen our life together. Though very different beings, we usually come to rest in mutual agreement regarding answers to life's big decisions. This isn't always present in the smaller moments, such as how much to feed the cat or when to stop at a yellow light and when to just speed through it. Yet despite these daily differences, our big decisions are grounded by a shared vision that makes it obvious which path to take. Whether it be to start a family, return to California, or create a school, from the start it has been this way: a simplicity of agreement on what feels right.

Our new chapters reveal themselves to be an extension of the story that began with a kiss on the neck. Arriving at the various summits of life together is immensely satisfying. The view is a good one, and it is a blessing to be accompanied.

# PART FOUR

# WISDOM
# THROUGH
# WANDERING

# A Mother's Advice

*"I slept and I dreamt that life was joy.*
*I awoke and saw that life was service.*
*I acted and behold, service was joy."*
– TAGORE

Eat together    Offer small kindnesses    Remember people's names

Sweat    Make friends with death    Stay limber

Drink water    Use only what you need    Forgive freely

Breathe    Give things away    Touch lovingly

Choose simple    Wear comfortable shoes    Do something different

Rest    Make your life your art    Listen to stillness

Serve others    Welcome what comes    Let love rule your life

# The Gift of Synchronicity

*"Respect your tight edges.*
*Work with them sensitively.*
*Lure them to greater openness."*
– ERICH SCHIFFMANN

W e are our own deepest mystery, and there is no one method for solving problems. In fact, sometimes we don't need to. Synchronicity's ability to deliver solutions is a gift I have come to rely on over the course of my lifetime. While I can't explain it, when I let go of fear and linger in uncertainty, I usually begin to see more clearly. I am most receptive when I don't have an answer for everything. Inspiration hovers more closely without my insistence upon a command performance, and certainly wisdom begins with an awareness of our own ignorance. It is the rare moment when we can stick our heads above the immeasurably complex flow of events and clearly witness the unfolding contours of our own lives. Sometimes the opportunity for this kind of clarity occurs at the exact moment when our situation feels impossibly complicated and even hopeless, just like my moment in Düsseldorf, collapsed on the couch with a baby in my arms. It is often in these difficult times that, by releasing our grip and relaxing, we receive the solution to our quandary. The next time you are feeling confused and uninspired, plant both of your feet firmly in unknowing and enjoy the spaciousness. Sometimes not knowing is the most honest and truthful place to rest. It takes courage not to have a plan. By relying on our capacities for patience and tolerance, an opening is created. Within this calm, a beautifully simple solution may be revealed.

# A Temporary Cure for Homesickness

*"Dependency blossoms into independence
in its own sweet time."*

– PEGGY O'MARA

A close cousin to heartbreak, homesickness is one of the potential hazards inherent in adventuring. Walking the cobblestone streets of Düsseldorf that first day, I recognized a familiar shadow marking its appearance with a tightening in my chest and catch in my breath. Loneliness was trailing along beside me, saying nothing. I was no stranger to homesickness, having suffered from it throughout my childhood. Spending the night at a friend's house often ended with my mother coming to retrieve me from the intended overnight, usually after a pleading phone call. But by this time in my life, I had learned about the three ingredients that keep homesickness at bay. They include place, project, and people.

## Ingredient #1: Place

The first thing to do is make a place for yourself. With Peter's house keys in my pocket, I marched up the four flights of terrazzo stairs to his flat, dragging my possessions behind me. The key fit smoothly into the black door, which opened onto a spacious hall washed with stripes of afternoon sun coming from the bedroom doorways. Peter had told me to make myself comfortable in the guestroom. Well-appointed, it was dove-gray and trimmed in white. The room had a gentleness to it, illuminated by the soft winter light coming through a large window overlooking the even grayer Rhine River.

Unpacking my bag was like welcoming old friends into this new home. I unfolded my favorite orange sarong and draped it across the white dresser. The brightness cheered me. Arranging my four necklaces on top of the sarong, I saw my face in the mirror. A firm believer in talking to myself out loud when no one is around, I offered a few words of encouragement to my anxious reflection. I continued to empty the duffle bag into the generous drawers that easily held the rest of my belongings. After placing my book and alarm clock on the bedside table, I ventured out of the bedroom to find the bathroom. There was only one. I didn't want to frighten Peter by taking over his entire home, so I tucked my green bag of toiletries under the sink. I could figure that part out later. Even if I would only be staying a short time, this was home for now.

I began to explore the rest of the apartment. At the end of the large entry, a second hallway, quite narrow and long, led to the kitchen. The tall, white walls of that hallway were a gallery of framed photographs, clearly ones Peter had collected from his various adventures. In one, he was navigating a wild river in his yellow kayak, his paddle held high over his head. Another image revealed a smiling family of five grown-up children gathered together on a couch along with what looked like their mother and father. A ponytailed Peter sat in the middle, wearing his signature denim work shirt and jeans.

Entering the kitchen, I felt a surge of happiness. A white marble table occupied one side of the room, upon it a generous bowl of lemons and a vase of bright orange tulips. A stove, sink, and small refrigerator lined the opposite wall, while above them shelves displayed neat stacks of white dishware. This was a real kitchen. It had everything necessary for making a simple meal. A flutter of possibility passed through me. Peter would be returning home with another houseguest by early evening. I had just enough time to find the farmer's market I had heard about and concoct something to welcome them.

## *Ingredient #2: Project*

The Carlsplatz outdoor market was only a few blocks away from Peter's apartment. Little did I know at the time how well I would get to know all of the different vendors whose carts and stalls filled the square that cold, winter afternoon. Smells of pickled herring, ripe cheese, freshly baked *Vollkornbrot,* and grilled Bratwurst greeted me before I even saw the colorful plaza teeming with local residents shopping for their evening meals. My plan was to make a warming dish that required only the most basic ingredients. I decided on the menu—comfort food from my time in Paris.

WINTER MENU

Baked Brie with toasted almonds served on crostinis and accompanied by a frisée salad dressed in lemon vinaigrette. To drink, my favorite: cold champagne.

Returning from the market I felt buoyant. For the moment, the shadowy specter of homesickness dissolved into the warmth of a kitchen and the joy of making something to share. I have learned that it takes time (honestly said, I think it takes a year) to truly feel at home in a new place. The small threads that begin to weave a recognizable pattern into each day are such a welcome relief from the unknown and unfamiliar. They often come unexpectedly. In that moment, they tumbled out of a grocery bag.

## *Ingredient #3: People*

That evening, Peter had to ring the doorbell because I had the key. I welcomed him and Aldo into the apartment while the buttery smell of baked Brie and toasted bread enticed us all to the kitchen. We opened the champagne and sat down to enjoy a simple supper. The feeling of home had found itself in the company of new friends.

# Mindful Anticipation

*"Confusion conditions activity, which conditions consciousness,*
*which conditions embodied personality, which conditions impact,*
*which conditions mood, which conditions craving,*
*which conditions clinging, which conditions becoming,*
*which conditions birth, which conditions aging and death."*

– THE BUDDHA

Anticipating the many needs of everyone in the family is an art. It is a central ingredient for an easy evening, morning, afternoon, airplane flight, visit to the dentist, haircut, or car trip, to name but a few. It comes with practice, and its addition into family life will alleviate stress, help to defuse potential land mines (emotional and otherwise), and cultivate an abiding sense of well-being and security for everyone involved. It simply cannot be overrated when it comes to making life with children easier.

Mindful anticipation means thinking about what might happen before it happens and considering what you can do to ease and even avoid problem situations before they turn into fights, tantrums, and crankiness resulting from hunger, fatigue, and physical discomfort. The patterns inherent in family life are defined by the simple acts of eating, sleeping, and caring for one another: those things that nourish us both physically and emotionally. Any of these situations, including playtime, mealtime, bath time, and bedtime have the potential to be delightful or disastrous, depending on how deeply they have been thought through beforehand. Being a parent requires choreography—imagining how to make daily situations flow as smoothly as possible in order to avoid stress. When integrated into our lives in a rhythmic and expected way, playtime, mealtime, bath time, and bedtime can support the needs of each individual and establish a sense of belonging and security. It means managing situations so everyone knows what to expect, which of course always includes the unexpected.

In the Waldorf tradition, teachers are encouraged to meditate daily on each of their students. They visualize a particular child and ask these questions: What does this child need the most in this moment? What can I do to meet these needs? What is this child struggling with? What aggravates this situation? How can I ease the struggle? As a parent or caring adult, we can ask ourselves the same questions regarding our children and our loved ones. By allowing ourselves the time to consider the challenges those around us are facing, we can better understand their needs and how we can be helpful.

Weekends at our house always meant a home full of children. By the time Friday rolled around, you all wanted to invite a friend or two to come for a sleepover. Of course each of you (and your friends) were ready to let loose and play, even though you were worn out from a busy week of school, homework, and after school activities. Peter and I, while happy to have a household full of children, were also tired and ready for a break. Going out for dinner sounded easy, but as we thought through all that it would include—the driving, making hungry children sit quietly at a table, spilled drinks, and keeping everyone entertained until the food arrived, this imagined scenario sounded less appealing. When anticipating these possible complexities, staying home and organizing a simple dinner, maybe even take-out, was certainly preferable for everyone. Piling you all into a warm bath and serving pizza and dessert while you splashed in the tub meant that my needs as a tired mother and your needs for a party were each answered. Getting you into clean pajamas afterwards and reading a story until you (and usually Peter and I) all fell fast asleep worked well for everyone, and it meant the next morning we would wake feeling well-rested and ready for whatever the day might hold.

Thinking ahead, paying attention to the emotional landscapes of family and home, and recognizing what situations are going to trigger conflict, fatigue, and restlessness become important strategies in maintaining an environment that is as stress-free as possible. The present moment becomes enhanced when we imagine in advance its potential for happiness.

# How to Breathe

*"As long as there is breath in the body, there is life.*
*When breath departs, so too does life.*
*Therefore, regulate the breath."*

– HATHA YOGA PRADIPIKA

It took me almost fifty years to learn how. The deeply satisfying experience of an absolutely complete breath was one that I enjoyed only occasionally, but not because I really knew what I was doing. It wasn't for lack of trying. I had been taking classes in Hatha yoga since I was a teenager. Some of them included instruction in the yogic art of breathing, pranayama. The benefits of the breath were clear. By learning how to control our respiratory system, we allow it to function at its best. I understood the basic biology: Oxygen nourishes the body and allows our cells to discharge the carbon dioxide accumulated in them. This automatically improves the circulatory system, without which the processes of digestion and elimination would suffer due to the accumulation of toxins. A full and relaxed breath is a signal to our central nervous system that everything is alright. Even with this understanding, I still had difficulty taking a deep breath. It often seemed to get caught somewhere in my throat.

I was starting to think it was just me. In yoga classes, I couldn't understand the complicated instructions that often accompanied an inhalation. Sometimes I would experience the enjoyment of a complete breath: that round fullness initiated from deep in the belly, the feeling of invisible nourishment rolling down behind my throat as it expanded into my lungs, then departed in a luxurious release through my nose. It always left in its wake a deep sense of peace. But it came unbidden, and I didn't know how to control it.

When I turned fifty, I attended a yoga workshop with a well-known teacher. At the beginning of the class, he asked if anyone had any questions in particular. I asked about how to breathe. He made some joke about it, saying I was probably in the wrong place if I didn't know how to do such a simple thing. I was extremely embarrassed and didn't stay for the afternoon class.

Returning home, I recounted the story to my friend Eliza, one of the most accomplished yoginis I know. She smiled and said, "You know about the tip of the nose approach, right?" I replied that I didn't know what she meant. She went on to explain: "Breathe through your nostrils, starting the breath from deep in your belly and focusing on the tip of your nose. Consciously bring your breath up and in through the tip of your nose." I tried it and was amazed. My breath didn't get caught in my throat. Instead, navigating with the clear image of nose tip, it rolled down through the trachea without a hitch. My lungs expanded and my heart felt a natural release with the culminating exhalation. I could breathe!

A full breath is not something that can be forced. Rather, it appears when welcomed. It can be enjoyed anywhere, anytime. Taking time to notice the breath cycle, it becomes clear that an inhalation increases energy while tightening and strengthening, and an exhalation releases energy, thus softening and lengthening. It is often helpful to match the length of the inhale with that of the exhale. The sum result is an overall feeling of well-being, grounded in stillness.

Once I am in this place of conscious breathing, I often enter into a Buddhist practice known as *tonglen*. Reversing our natural tendency to avoid suffering of any kind, the practice of tonglen asks us instead to embrace it. Beginning with an inhalation, we breathe in all of the suffering that surrounds us, including our own. Breathing out, we send joy, relief, and happiness to all beings. When I practice tonglen, I feel like a human air purifier, breathing in the world's sorrow and breathing out a cloud of golden light. This practice has the power to open our hearts while helping us to overcome our fear of suffering. It allows breath to become a bridge, connecting us to ourselves and others. We breathe in for all of life; we breathe out for all of life.

# Thanksgiving Meets the Eightfold Path

*"The aim is to bring fresh awareness into everything we do.
Whether walking or standing still, sitting or lying down . . .
awareness is a process of deepening self-acceptance . . .
whatever it observes it embraces.
There is nothing unworthy of acceptance.*

— STEPHEN BATCHELOR

Wouldn't it be helpful if life came with operating instructions? Even a toaster comes with an owner's manual. There are a few things we can be sure of, and at the top of that list is: Change happens no matter what. This is the very difficult truth about living and loving on this earth. Being alive is challenging for everyone. The Buddha was right when he said that life is suffering. The cause of this suffering is pretty straightforward: it's us. Our minds struggle in response to the impermanent nature of existence. There is, however, some good news. Buddha didn't just leave us in a soup of hopelessness. The teachings of a monk who lived over 2,500 years ago in a completely different time and place still ring true today. The suggested practices of the Eightfold Path offer an opportunity to understand and enjoy each moment, despite its complexity and uncertainty. I know that sometimes without concrete examples, it can be difficult to understand how to employ these practices. Sure, they sound good on paper, but how do they relate to our day-to-day living?

Ten years ago we instigated what has become our traditional Thanksgiving celebration. Every year Peter and I invite the entire Buckley family to come and spend the day together. The Buckley clan is a large one, and often as many as thirty or forty relatives and friends gather at our home for an afternoon and evening of reconnecting with one another and enjoying a traditional Thanksgiving dinner. Even though our guests generously bring their signature dishes, it still means a lot of organizing and cooking for Peter and me. As much as I enjoy gathering the family, the occasion has the potential to make me frantic. I have more than once forgotten to enjoy myself in my efforts to accomplish everything. It's easy to overlook what holds real importance when there are so many little tasks that need doing. The point of the holiday is not the tasks, but I become so busy being busy that I rarely land in the beauty and happiness of the occasion. So this year, I decided to incorporate Buddha's eight suggestions to relieve suffering, with the hope that I could slow down and honestly enjoy what was directly in front of me. It really worked. His advice helped me to pay attention and find pleasure both in the making of the day as well as the gathering of family. While this is a very simple example, I believe the perspectives offered by the Eightfold Path can help us navigate even the most difficult and painful situations. Starting with a relatively easy one like Thanksgiving was good practice, and I now give thanks for the Buddha's wise and practical advice.

## A Thanksgiving Recipe

### 1. WISE UNDERSTANDING

The first thing I needed to do was to admit that I wasn't having much fun. While it appeared that everyone else thoroughly enjoyed the family Thanksgiving, I was often left with the feeling of having missed out on something. In my worst moments, I couldn't find pleasure in even the simplest tasks, nor did I allow myself the time to engage in genuine conversation with other family members. Buddha asks us to recognize the cause of our suffering. He explains that it resides in our response to the inevitability of change—in the fact that nothing is in our control and everything is impermanent. When you consider this truth, it is fairly unsettling. It's no wonder we prefer not to notice it. I had kept myself busy because I felt less vulnerable. I didn't realize that by acknowledging the fact that nothing lasts forever, everything and everyone become just that much more precious. It was time to reconsider my actions. I realized I was behaving in an unconscious way. I wasn't paying attention to what was happening around me. Instead of recognizing how valuable an opportunity it is to gather with family and friends, I was busying myself (in a slightly irritable way) with organizing. So, I made a decision. I would slow down, notice, and enjoy. I would make time to connect with family and catch up as much as I could with each individual, even if it was only a brief conversation. I would give thanks.

## 2. WISE INTENTION

Once I understood how I had created my own unhappiness, I knew I probably wasn't alone. When we pay attention to our own suffering and comprehend the cause, it becomes easy to recognize the unhappiness of those around us. Social occasions, especially those including family, can bring up all sorts of issues. There was a good chance others at the gathering were also struggling in their own ways. Buddha explains that Wise Intention means to purpose our daily lives with the intent to lessen suffering in this world. Witnessing the plight of others becomes our motivation for compassionate action. It certainly spurred me on. I made an intention to genuinely connect with others. I also made an intention to check in with myself. If I needed a moment of escape, I could prepare the whipped cream or fill the water glasses. I reminded myself that everything is fragile; all of this could, and eventually would, disappear. I embraced the whirlwind of activity, knowing I would miss it if it wasn't there. I enjoyed becoming overwhelmed by the beauty of the occasion and the bounty of the world.

## 3. WISE SPEECH

I am not from the school of sticks and stones. I believe words can hurt as much as they can heal. On the occasion of Thanksgiving, I made an extra effort to reach out and tell friends and loved ones how important they are to me and how grateful I am for their presence in my life. Others did the same for me, and it meant so much to hear their kind words. Their love supported me in my effort to be more open, aware, and vulnerable. One of my favorite teachers said that there are only three sentences that are necessary in this world: I'm sorry. Thank you. I love you.

### 4. WISE ACTION

Not getting lost in unimportant details, attuning myself to the situation at hand, and allowing events to unfold without force brought relief from my previous behavior. Noticing the needs of those around me and attending to them was enjoyable. I recognized that every moment offers yet another chance to take a full breath and drop in to the present. Wise Action results in awareness, and awareness results in wise action.

### 5. WISE LIVELIHOOD

Originally, Thanksgiving was a holiday that celebrated the harvest and the bounty of the earth. In this culture of consumption, the economy of the natural systems that support all of life is precarious at best. We are now using the resources of one-and-a-half planets on our one and only planet. Buddha describes Wise Livelihood as being able to support and provide for ourselves and those around us in a wholesome way that is not exploitive. This includes being aware of the environmental cost of our needs and thinking twice before buying anything. It isn't easy, especially because shopping has become an avenue for creative expression and social connection in our culture. I needed to do a lot of shopping to prepare for Thanksgiving. By slowing down and remembering the consequences of consuming, I was able to make better decisions regarding what we honestly needed.

### 6. WISE EFFORT

Staying awake at the wheel isn't always easy, especially when everyone is talking, drinking, and consuming carbohydrates. This is where Wise

Effort comes in. Buddha describes this as cultivating skillful and peaceful mind habits. Wise Effort identifies that part of ourselves which is constant and that part which is reactive. It's a good idea to cultivate this understanding outside of the daily hustle and bustle. I like to quiet my mind with the help of deep breaths until I land on my own inner bedrock of stillness. Returning to this place on a regular basis makes it easier to access when I am in a stressful situation where emotions are flying all around. Instead of blurting out any thought that comes into my head or making an indiscriminate decision, I call upon the calm that I know to be my core. From this vantage point, I can navigate complicated moments in life more skillfully.

## 7. WISE CONCENTRATION

It might happen as I am stringing the green beans, peeling the potatoes, or at the end of the evening when faced with the dirty dishes piled high in the sink. Amidst what your grandmother Peggie calls "heavenly bedlam," a moment will appear when I can give thanks. This is a time when I have the opportunity to recall all of the kindnesses each person has shown me, when I can appreciate myself for behaving well, and remember all of the people I love who aren't in the room and perhaps are no longer in this world. It is a moment of gratitude, because there is always something to be grateful for.

## 8. WISE MINDFULNESS

Even with the best of intentions, it isn't always possible to have a meaningful conversation with everyone at our Thanksgiving gathering. To remedy this, we allow time at the end of the evening to hear individual stories. After dinner, our family and friends retire to the comfy living room and sit in a big circle. We choose a topic for the evening that allows plenty of personal interpretation. This year the theme was "And then I realized ..." As we went around the circle, each person recounted a story that included a moment of realization or awakening. The stories, all very different, described an instance when recognition of a new awareness occurred. Each story mirrored an experience of mindfulness. Wise Mindfulness is about supporting the awareness of our own experience and behavior, as well as the impact we have upon others. Being mindful means paying attention. It gets easier with practice, and it sure makes for a happy Thanksgiving.

# Invite Beauty

*"Let the beauty we love be what we do.*
*There are hundreds of ways*
*to kneel and kiss the ground."*

– RUMI

Beauty is free. It exists the moment we choose to care about something. There is a holy day in the Hindu tradition where the tools used in daily life are celebrated. On colorful cloths surrounded by garlands of marigolds, the merchants, artisans, and householders display all of the utensils they use in their various professions and everyday life. Each item has been polished, sharpened, and cleaned for this special holiday. Candles and sticks of incense are lit in honor of the implements that make possible all of the different livelihoods. The tools and the people who use them enjoy a day off together.

There is something wonderful about acknowledging the importance of those things which are so necessary to us, whether it be a broom, shovel, or a paintbrush. In this honoring, they become objects of beauty. Treating a home with this same kind of care and recognition imbues it with an inviting sense of welcome and calm. Even the smallest room can become a place of spaciousness if the objects within it are cared for and valued.

Because of our busy lives, it is only natural that our home, along with our possessions, invite chaos. Clutter, besides making it difficult to remember where anything is, encourages more clutter. Plunging into a mess and emerging organized on the other side, I experience a simple happiness and even an internal lightness. Finding that previously buried book or something I had forgotten about in my closet can become a surprising source of inspiration. I feel less encumbered knowing what I have and where it is. I have found that when you model the practice of caring for your possessions and valuing beauty, those around you, including children, will learn to do the same. You don't even need to require them to do it, as they will internalize the feeling that accompanies an organized home. Even if it isn't apparent during their childhood and adolescent years, they will eventually bring this same appreciation into their own lives later on. Cultivating beauty, even if only by picking up trash, is an expression of respect for life itself. Whether it be in the form of a pristine beach, an arrangement of flowers, or a genuine expression of kindness, beauty honors life.

# Make Friends with Stillness

*"Within you there is a stillness and a sanctuary*
*to which you can retreat at any time and be yourself."*
– HERMANN HESSE

Every place we choose to inhabit reflects who we are. We surround ourselves with objects that hold meaning for us and perhaps tell a story of our lives. Although they might be pleasing things, it is not their intrinsic loveliness, intrigue, or aesthetics that warms a living space and makes it the place where we feel at ease. This feeling of connectivity and welcome is a direct reflection of how at home we feel within ourselves. It is this inner belonging that allows us to create a congruency with the world surrounding us. Our interior lives then become a bridge to the outer world. But where does this feeling come from? How do we find it?

Stillness offers a place where we can understand this experience of connection. I once listened to a meditation teacher describe the attainment of inner stillness as similar to watching a glass of unfiltered apple juice settle after it has been poured. It takes several moments for the residue to slowly come to rest and allow the clarity of the juice to reveal itself. When we let our personal stories, moods, concerns, and preferences settle, we land in a deeper part of our being. From this place of stillness, we can view life without the usual hubbub of continuously arising thoughts and emotions. When we stop reacting to everything around us and become a witness to our own selves, we experience a deep calm. This is what the Buddhists call calm abiding; we see the world as a baby sees it, aware of everything all at once, without conscious selection and interpretation.

From this viewpoint, we notice ourselves as being part of a much greater whole. In stillness, with our minds at rest, we witness ourselves without judgment. We feel our core being as something more than our current mind state, regardless of whether it be comfortable or uncomfortable. In fact, we become familiar with the habits of mind that can cause suffering (comparison, judgment, anger, annoyance, and fear to name a few) without identifying with them. In noticing this pattern, we begin to understand that the mind is often operating with or without our approval. It loves to tell stories, solve problems, and invent new ideas. In addition, it can also judge harshly, become agitated, and create separation. This is simply the nature of our minds.

I know you've heard the word mindfulness before. Being mindful means noticing your own emotional habits, including the ones that cause confusion and unhappiness. When you are experiencing a difficult situation or complicated feelings, assume the role of a witness. By doing so, you can identify these emotions and see them as separate from your inner being, that part of you that exists before you have a thought. Experiencing your state of mind from this perspective allows you the freedom to choose how you want to respond. It might just be that you let any feelings of sadness, anger, or worry pass over like clouds in the sky. You can be sure with time they will depart. One thing we all can count on is change.

Once, while sitting with my thoughts during a ten-day silent meditation retreat, I realized there were about seven different recordings my mind would play, including Am I Good Enough?, When is Lunch? (also known as Foods that I Love), and What I Am Going to Do When I Get Home. These same thoughts had been completely dominating my experience since the beginning of the retreat. After six days of listening to each one over and over, they became recognizable. Noticing this allowed me to gently quiet these thoughts. When they arrived unbidden,

I would say thank you for their concern and interest and breathe them out into stillness. For a few seconds at a time I was finally able to rest without interruption and notice the present moment, which for me was life changing. It was an experience of freedom. And of course, after a few breaths, the next thought would appear. But during those brief interludes when I found respite from my own inner chattering, I also found something else. I found me. Allowing my thoughts to settle, I felt deeply at home.

The capacity to act with loving kindness flourishes when grounded in this understanding. When I escape from the habits of judgment and reactivity, my spirit becomes buoyant and expansive. I feel kinder toward myself and everyone around me. The restorative and spacious expanse of stillness offers a sanctuary for our spirits. Living into this, if only for a few breaths each day, is a great habit to incorporate into our lives.

# Practice Balance

Almost every Saturday evening of my childhood I was invited to spend the night at my grandparents' home. I would awake to the sound of my grandfather in the kitchen making his famous Sunday morning hotcakes. Racing downstairs, I would sometimes stop to see my grandmother, then in her seventies. I still have a vivid memory of bursting into their bedroom and seeing her sprawled across the floor in her lavender yoga outfit. She had been practicing her headstand against the door I had unknowingly thrown open. She looked surprised but smiled and explained to me what she was doing. Inviting me in, she then began to teach me various yoga poses, the most memorable being the Simha asana, or Lion's pose. Watching my elegant grandmother bellowing with her tongue stuck out was unforgettable.

My grandmother's yoga practice didn't seem so unusual at the time, although yoga had not yet become as mainstream as it is today. My mother has had a daily yoga practice for years, and my father began every day with a run and a swim. As I grew up, I learned by their examples how deeply connected a healthy physical body is to our overall sense of well-being. Taking care of your body is a way of being kind to yourself.

We are given the gift of body, mind, and spirit, and all three need to be appreciated and nurtured. Attending to the health of each one can feel like a juggling act, but it is a skill worth cultivating. Self-discipline allows you the opportunity to put your ideas into action, accomplish your dreams, and inspire others. Exercising the mind is valuable not only because it is good for it, but also because it enlivens your natural curiosity and keeps you interested and interesting. Once, in a conversation with your grandmother (who was ninety at the time) I said, "You know Mom, it feels just as satisfying to work hard doing something you love as it does to play hard." Without hesitation she responded, "Better!" It does seem to be true. One effort enjoys the complementary balance of the other, and maintaining this balance is an expression of respect for life itself.

# How to Accompany the Dying

*"To die will be an awfully big adventure."*
– PETER PAN

Every Thursday for six years I offered massage to the residents at the Zen Hospice in San Francisco. This experience allowed me to cultivate a relationship with the process of dying and to alleviate my own fears around death. Frank Ostaseski is the founder of Zen Hospice Project and the Metta Institute. One of my favorite remarks he often made was, "Death is not an emergency." After the moment of death, time is abundant. Frank developed these Five Precepts "as companions on the journey of accompanying the dying." Having spent nearly three decades focusing on the practices of mindful and compassionate hospice care, Frank offers these precepts which truly are an invaluable gift of practical wisdom.

## Five Precepts by Frank Ostaseski

A while back, I developed five precepts as companions on the journey of accompanying the dying. Perhaps they have relevance in other dimensions of life and can offer some inspiration and guidance. I think of these as five bottomless practices that can be continually explored and deepened. They are not linear and have no value as theories or concepts. To be understood and realized, they have to be lived into and communicated through action.

THE FIRST PRECEPT: *Welcome Everything. Push Away Nothing.*

In welcoming everything, we don't have to like what's arising. It's actually not our job to approve or disapprove. It's our task to trust, listen, and to pay careful attention to the changing experience. At the deepest level, we are being asked to cultivate a kind of fearless receptivity.

This is a journey of continuous discovery in which we will always be entering new territory. We have no idea how it will turn out, and it takes courage and flexibility. We find balance. The journey is a mystery we need to live into—opening, risking, and forgiving constantly.

THE SECOND PRECEPT: *Bring Your Whole Self to the Experience.*

In the process of healing others and ourselves we open to both our joy and fear. In the service of this healing we draw on our strength and helplessness, our wounds and passion to discover a meeting place with the other. Professional warmth doesn't heal. It is not our expertise but the exploration of our own suffering that enables us to be of real assistance. That's what allows us to touch another human being's pain with compassion instead of fear and pity. We have to invite it all in. We can't travel with others in territory that we haven't explored ourselves. It is the exploration of our own inner life that enables us to form an empathetic bridge to the other person.

THE THIRD PRECEPT: *Don't Wait.*

Patience is different than waiting. When we wait, we are full of expectations. When we're waiting, we miss what the moment has to offer. Worrying or strategizing about what the future holds for us, we miss the opportunities that are right in front of us. Waiting for the moment of death, we miss so many moments of living. Don't wait. If there's someone you love, tell him or her that you love them. Allow the precarious nature of this life to show you what's most important. Then enter fully.

THE FOURTH PRECEPT: *Find a Place to Rest in the Middle of Things.*

We often think of rest as something that will come when everything else is complete, like when we go on a holiday or when our work is done. We imagine that we can only find rest by changing the conditions of our life. But it is possible to discover rest right in the middle of chaos. It is experienced when we bring our full attention, without distraction, to this moment, to this activity. This place of rest is always available. We need only turn toward it. It's an aspect of us that's never sick, is not born, and does not die.

THE FIFTH PRECEPT: *Cultivate Don't Know Mind.*

This describes a mind that's open and receptive. A mind that's not limited by agendas, roles, and expectations. The great Zen teacher, Suzuki Roshi, was fond of saying, "In the beginner's mind there are many possibilities, but in the expert's mind there are few."

From this vantage point we realize that "not knowing is most intimate." Understanding this we stay very close to the experience allowing the situation itself to inform our actions. We listen carefully to our own inner voice, sensing our urges, trusting our intuition. We learn to look with fresh eyes.

– FRANK OSTASESKI

# Recipe for Loving Kindness

*"Forget your perfect offering.*
*There is a crack, a crack in everything.*
*That's how the light gets in."*
– LEONARD COHEN

I had counted her as a dear friend, never imagining this would happen. Unexpectedly, she withdrew from our relationship of fifteen years, dismissing all the love and affection we had shared. I was bereft; I didn't know what to do with all the sadness I felt. That's when the practice of Metta came to the rescue. I had learned about Metta several years before during a Buddhist Vipassana retreat. While I appreciated the intention behind the practice, I hadn't really integrated it into my own life. I didn't know how effective it could be. But now, suffering from this particular sadness of lost friendship and seeming betrayal, I turned to loving kindness as a cure.

Everyone and everything thrives on kindness. Metta is a Pali word commonly translated in English as loving kindness. Metta practice, in its essence, is a strong wish for the happiness of both ourselves and others. It fosters forgiveness, and in my experience, can heal a broken heart. Just like taking a full breath, Metta can be practiced almost anywhere at any time. Perhaps you are on a long drive, waiting for someone, taking a walk, or about to fall asleep. You don't need a lot of time or a special place to cultivate this practice. I decided to devote ten minutes every day to it, with the hopes that it would allow for some kind of clarity.

Here's how the practice was explained to me: To begin, take a few moments to quiet your mind. Enjoy a full breath or two and begin to focus your attention on the experience of loving kindness. You can start off by offering Metta to yourself. Simply recite the following phrases:

> May I be safe and protected.
> May I be peaceful and happy.
> May I be healthy and filled with love.
> May I be free of all suffering.

Sometimes it is just as hard to offer loving kindness to ourselves as it is to someone we dislike. Feelings of aversion or indecisiveness are not a failing. Rather, they are an opportunity to recognize and understand ourselves more fully. After a time, you will be able to release those negative emotions that lead to suffering. Don't worry about these feelings; simply notice them and relax. Once you feel complete with yourself, offer the wish of Metta to a loved one. When this feels grounded and fluid, begin to include in your practice one or more of the following categories of persons to whom you will offer Metta:

> *A close friend*
> *A neutral person*
> *A difficult person (Only go as close as is comfortable,*
> *replacing negative feelings with Metta.)*

> May you/s/he/it be safe and protected.
> May you/s/he/it be peaceful and happy.
> May you/s/he/it be healthy and filled with love.
> May you/s/he/it be free of all suffering.

Traditionally, the practice ends with offering Metta to all beings.

In the beginning, I found it especially difficult to offer unconditional love to someone who had hurt me. I remembered being instructed not to force it, so instead I simply sat with all of the feelings and emotions that arose. They spilled out in myriad ways, and I didn't know if I would ever be free of them. Slowly, little by little, I was able to incrementally release small pieces of the sadness and anger that had burrowed into my heart. And then something really interesting happened. One afternoon, about three weeks into dedicating myself to the practice, a shift occurred. As I conjured up an image of her in my mind, instead of my usual feelings of anger and grief, I experienced a clearing of emotion. I saw her as she is: beautiful, intelligent, and incredibly fun to be with. I also saw her wounds: the immense suffering she had experienced during her childhood in the hands of an extremely abusive mother. I understood my role in unknowingly activating those wounds, and most importantly, that her response to me was, in fact, not personal. Rather, it was a result of bonding patterns that had been established long before our friendship. I experienced a rush of compassion for her and also for myself. I understood the problem. I could release her with love and begin to let go of my sorrow.

Having experienced the healing power of Metta, I use it whenever I feel out of sorts with myself or someone else. While it is true that time heals an aching heart, Metta practice opens up an avenue that allows us to understand our own suffering. It also offers an opportunity to witness, at our own pace, the suffering of others. Seeing this condition clearly, our desire for the world and all living creatures to find freedom from pain and sorrow naturally arises. Filling ourselves with Metta, we wish the world well.

> May you be safe and protected.
> May you be peaceful and happy.
> May you be healthy and filled with love.
> May you be free of all suffering.

# Just Add Water

Peter and I were married on it. Your father was a master of diving into it. You lived in it before your first breath. It soothed the contractions that delivered you. You've been comfortable in it since your birth, when the midwife washed you in its warmth. You played nightly in a tub of it, styling one another with bubble hairdos. We used it to put out fires and encourage newly planted seeds. We deemed it sacred, scattering it in a circle at the beginning of festivals. We have lived by it, listened to it, and learned from it. It has taught us to dance around obstacles with grace and has filled our view with a blue tranquility. We used it to wash your grandfather's body and then relied on it to carry his ashes. We have played in it endlessly, on boards and boats, rafts and kayaks. It has frightened us with its power and soothed us with its presence. We have tried to capture it in drawings, photographs, stories, and songs. Like our planet, we are mainly composed of it. We choose to reunite with one another in its presence. As a family we share the same love affair. Water is our teacher, and we are at home in its presence. When we just add water, we experience ourselves as complete. This connection wordlessly reminds us of our own belonging. We are here. We are together. We are love.

# PART FIVE

# SOUPMAKING
# AND SOULMAKING
## *Family Recipes*

# Granny's Fresh Pea Soup

If grandmothers ruled the world, surely shelling peas would be their secret weapon for peace. Learning to make pea soup would be obligatory in school. The reason? Perhaps it's the neighborly feeling a pod reveals when opened: how thoroughly contented the small peas appear, so perfectly snuggled together. Mining the contents found in a generous bowl of pods invites conversation—the completed task leaving everyone with a sense of accomplishment and well-being. When grandmothers rule the world, there will be an official global holiday for making pea soup, ensuring everyone a delicious dinner and a peaceful planet.

MAKES 6 CUPS OF SOUP

6 tablespoons unsalted butter
1½ cups diced yellow onion (about 2 medium onions)
½ teaspoon freshly grated nutmeg
1 teaspoon salt
3 cups shelled English peas, from 3 pounds in the pod
4 cups stock (either vegetable or chicken)
1 teaspoon granulated sugar
salt and freshly ground pepper, to taste

GARNISH
6 teaspoons Greek nonfat yogurt
6 large mint leaves, cut carefully into thin ribbons

1. Heat a large saucepan over high heat for about 1 minute. Add the butter, and when it foams, stir in the onion, nutmeg, and 1 teaspoon of salt. Turn down the heat to medium and cook 5–7 minutes, until the onion is translucent and just starting to color.

2. Add the peas, ½ cup of stock, and sugar. Stir to coat well. Cook another 4–5 minutes, until the peas turn bright green and tender.

3. Put half of the pea mixture into a blender or food processor and blend for 2 minutes. Next, add 1½ cups of stock and blend for another minute, until completely smooth. Pour into a large saucepan. Repeat the process with remaining pea mixture. The additional stock may be added if the soup appears too thick. Stir mixture and season to taste with salt and pepper.

4. Soup can be served cold or hot, each bowl or cup garnished with a spoonful of yogurt and a scattering of sliced mint over the top.

# Peggie's Chocolate Crackle Cookies

The doctor laughed at her complaint. Your grandmother, Peggie, was in for her annual check-up. Although approaching her ninety-fourth birthday, Peggie has always been someone whose adventurous spirit and love of life propels her into the most unusual situations. At this very moment, she might be riding a camel somewhere in the desert to visit the Great Pyramids or zip-lining across a forest canopy in a Costa Rican jungle.

Her latest trip had been with us on the garden isle of Kauai. Hanalei Bay was a relatively quiet destination compared to her usual jaunts, but Peggie decided to spice it up by taking up surfing. Every afternoon she would put on her brightly colored bathing suit and flowered swimming cap, grab a boogie board, and walk out to the beach with Peter. Helping her out past the gentle breakers, Peter would stand behind her while they waited for the next set. When the perfect wave appeared he would give her a big push, and amidst screams of delight, she would ride it all the way into shore.

The result of all this activity was that, upon returning home, she had a few sore muscles. When the doctor asked her how she was feeling, she mentioned this fact. He naturally asked why, and when she explained that she had just returned from a surf trip, he wasn't exactly sympathetic. In fact, he couldn't stop laughing and sent her home with a clean bill of health.

Peggie is often asked about her vibrant longevity. How does she maintain her quick-witted, sure-footed, elegant presence? Her response will always include a shrug and a smile, perhaps crediting the love she has for her family or the health benefits of martinis. I have always held the theory that it has something to do with her Chocolate Crackle Cookies.

MAKES ABOUT 6 DOZEN COOKIES

2 cups unbleached white flour
2 teaspoons baking powder
¼ teaspoon salt
4 ounces unsweetened chocolate, melted
½ cup vegetable oil
2 cups granulated sugar
4 eggs
2 teaspoons vanilla
1 pound of confectioners' sugar

1. Sift together flour, baking powder, and salt.

2. Blend melted chocolate, vegetable oil, and sugar in a large bowl. Add the eggs one at a time, mixing thoroughly. Stir in vanilla.

3. Add flour mixture to wet ingredients and combine all. Cover bowl and refrigerate at least 2 hours or overnight.

4. Adjust oven rack to lower one third of the oven. Preheat to 350 degrees.

5. Pour confectioners' sugar into plastic bag. Roll dough into balls the size of walnuts and drop in bag to coat. Place dough balls on parchment lined baking sheets an inch and a half apart and bake 10 minutes—do not overcook. They will firm when cooled.

# Dragon's Breath Ginger Tea

It is nearly impossible to give an exact recipe for ginger tea because there are so many variables. Are you adding honey, sugar, agave, or a combination of these? Mexican ginger or Hawaiian ginger? Regular lemons, Meyer lemons, or a combo of limes and lemons? All of these options will make a difference, and none of them are wrong. My favorite lemons to use are the Meyers, which give the tea a wonderful taste when combined with orange blossom honey. I prefer the larger Hawaiian ginger, as it has less of a bite than its smaller cousin, usually grown in Mexico.

Whatever combination of ingredients you use, the trick is to be generous with both the sweetener and the lemon juice, finding the balance between the two. The result will be a delicious pot of Dragon's Breath Tea. Besides tasting good, it can help with the prevention of colds, calm an upset stomach, and even ease morning sickness. Serve it hot or cold, garnished with a fresh mint leaf. It will keep up to three weeks in the refrigerator, or you can freeze it until ready to use.

MAKES 45 SERVINGS

12 quarts of cold water
6 cups of fresh ginger, rinsed and sliced into thin rounds
    (no need to peel)
2–3 cups of lemon juice
2–3 cups of honey/sugar
fresh mint leaves as garnish

1. Fill your 12-quart pot (probably the one you use to boil spaghetti) with fresh water. Add the ginger and put the pot on the stove over high heat. Bring ginger and water to a boil, then turn down the heat, maintaining a gentle simmer for up to 1 hour. The longer you boil it, the stronger the brew. After you turn off the heat, let it cool slightly before adding the sweeteners.

2. Stir to blend. Add in your lemon juice first, mixing thoroughly. Next, add the first two cups of sweetener and taste. You can use only honey or part sugar and part honey, depending on your preference. Continue to slowly add sweetener until it really tastes good to you. It generally will taste a little less sweet once it has completely cooled.

3. When it does cool completely (the ginger will sink to the bottom), strain with a large, fairly fine strainer into your pitchers, teapots, and containers. If you want an extra strong brew, leave it in the pot (with a lid on) overnight, preferably somewhere cool, and strain the next morning. If the tea tastes too strong, simply adjust it by adding water. Ginger tea is not fragile, so don't be afraid to make it taste just the way you like it. Enjoy!

# Cho's Special Noodles

Everyone loves Cho's noodles. Born in Korea, Sung Ja Cho learned to make these noodles from her mother. The Korean name for this dish is Chop Che. Whenever we celebrated a festival with our school community, Cho would generously prepare a large bowl of these noodles for the potluck. Light and delicious, they were always the first dish to disappear from the table.

SERVES 15 PEOPLE
(BUT BE WARNED;
IT WON'T LAST LONG!)

2 dozen dried shiitake mushrooms
2 bunches of fresh spinach
3 bell peppers (red, yellow, and orange in color)
1 large yellow onion
3–4 peeled carrots
1 bunch green onions
2 cloves garlic, peeled
1 tablespoon fresh ginger, minced
3–4 tablespoons toasted sesame oil
1 teaspoon salt
3 tablespoons ground toasted sesame seeds (Make these fresh
    by toasting in a hot frying pan. Let cool, then grind.)
3–4 tablespoons vegetable oil
5 tablespoons soy sauce
2 teaspoons sugar

1 large bag (500 grams) Korean Chop Che noodles. These are made from purple yams and can be purchased at most Asian markets. They are long and semi-translucent.

2 tablespoons whole sesame seeds, toasted

1. Soak dried mushrooms in bowl of warm water for 1 hour.

2. Fill pot (5 quart saucepan is big enough) with cold water and put on the stove to boil for cooking the spinach.

3. Wash the spinach (leave stems on) and plunge into boiling water for two minutes. Be careful not to overcook. As Cho says, "Too soft not so good; stay a little bit crispy." Strain spinach and rinse under cold water until cool. Squeeze all of the extra water out of the spinach with your hands and form two balls. Set aside on a baking tray or platter. Fill the same pot with water and put it back on the stove to boil, as you will be cooking the noodles in it later.

4. Remove the core and seeds from the bell peppers and slice lengthwise into thin strips. Set aside on the baking tray or platter alongside the spinach.

5. Skin, then cut the yellow onion in half lengthwise through the root end, and then cut each half crosswise into fairly thin slices, similar in size to the bell peppers. Add to tray, keeping separate.

6. Cut each peeled carrot into diagonal rounds, and then, holding the rounds together, slice thinly into matchstick size pieces. Add to tray with onions.

7. Cut green onions into diagonal 1-inch pieces. Add to tray, keeping separate.

8. Peel 2 cloves of garlic and mince finely. Mix minced ginger and garlic together and set aside.

9. The mushrooms should be ready by this time. Remove them from the water, and cut stems off at the base and discard. Cut each mushroom into ¼-inch wide strips. After all have been cut, gather up a

handful and squeeze them hard, removing any extra water. You will end up with several handfuls. Add to tray, keeping separate.

10. Have ready a large bowl to hold the finished salad. Put spinach balls on the cutting board and slice through them several times; then add to bowl. Mix spinach together with 1 tablespoon toasted sesame oil, ¼ teaspoon salt, and 1 tablespoon toasted ground sesame seeds. Set aside.

11. Heat a large frying pan on the stove over high heat, then add 1 tablespoon of vegetable oil. Add all of the sliced peppers and stir to coat. Add 1 tablespoon of soy sauce and ¼ teaspoon of salt. Cook for 2 minutes, stirring frequently. Put into the large bowl with the spinach. Peppers should be al dente. (How do you say that in Korean?)

12. Return pan to the stove over high heat. Add 1 tablespoon vegetable oil and ¼ teaspoon salt. Add the onions and carrots. Cook 2 minutes stirring frequently. Add them to the bowl with the peppers and spinach.

13. Return frying pan to the stove over high heat. Add 1 tablespoon of toasted sesame oil along with 1½ tablespoons soy sauce and 1 teaspoon sugar. Add the mushrooms and stir. If the mushrooms haven't soaked long enough and seem too chewy, you can add a dash of water and cook them a bit longer in the pan to soften. Taste them to decide if they are ready. When they are done, add them to the bowl with the rest of the vegetables.

14. Return pan to the stove over high heat one last time. Add a scant tablespoon of vegetable oil and then the green onions. Cook for 1 minute, stirring constantly. Add them to the bowl with all of the other vegetables, and mix them together thoroughly.

15. Add the entire package of noodles to boiling water along with a dash of toasted sesame oil. Boil for 5–7 minutes, stirring occasionally. Do not overcook! Once again, think al dente. Pour into a large strainer or colander with small holes. Cut across the noodles several times with a large pair of scissors.

16. Add noodles to the bowl with all of the veggies along with 2 tablespoons of toasted, whole sesame seeds, 2–3 tablespoons soy sauce, 1 tablespoon toasted sesame oil, 1 teaspoon sugar, and garlic-ginger mixture. Mix together well, and let cool. This noodle salad is best served warm or at room temperature and will keep in the refrigerator for three days—if it lasts that long!

# Peter's Tarte Tatin

E ach year, Coleman knew when his birthday was close because of the apples. The four craggy trees that ringed the garden would be laden with fruit. Old heirloom varieties, they offered tart green ones with thick skins and large red ones that would roll down the hill and under the fence to the delight of deer and raccoons. Crispy, sweet, yellow ones hung low to the ground, behind which the Pink Pearls, everyone's favorite, bashfully hid themselves. The Belle de Boskopp was known as the best baking apple. It held its shape when cooked, refusing to collapse amidst high heat, sugar, and butter—requisites for Peter's famous Tarte Tatin. Here is the recipe in his words:

It's all about the apples. You are not likely to find Belle de Boskopp, but Golden Delicious do well. You will find that apples "in season" hold up to cooking much better than the same apples "out of season." I use enough apples to fill the pan plus an inch because they cook down. A 9-inch cast-iron frying pan is cool, but I use a copper pan that has a frying pan shape (without the handle). A Tarte Tatin in Paris would use fewer apples and come out lower. Sometimes I cut the apples into quarters, chunky style, and sometimes into eighths.

MAKES 1 TARTE

8–10 apples, peeled, cored, and sliced
1½ cups sugar
3–4 tablespoons of unsalted butter
pastry (You can make a flaky pastry, but I just buy
    frozen puff pastry.)

1 lemon, juice and zest
ground cinnamon (optional)—not very French . . .
    but who cares?

1. Preheat oven to 400 degrees.

2. Place apple slices in a bowl. Sprinkle zest, ½ cup sugar, and lemon juice over them and toss. Let them sit for 30 minutes to drain. (Sugar makes them exude juice.) Meanwhile . . .

CARAMEL

1. Melt butter in the frying pan. Add 1 cup of sugar and cook over high heat until bubbly brown, about 4–5 minutes. Try to cook until you get a darker brown, but watch out that you don't burn the sugar. Remove from heat and let cool a minute or so.

2. Artistically place the first layer of apples on the bottom and sides (recall that the bottom becomes the top), and then loosely add the rest. Place back over medium-high heat and cook for 10–12 minutes while basting the buttery-caramel liquid over the apples until they soften a bit (partially cover to help soften). Remove from the heat.

3. Place pastry top over the entire pan, trim sides, cut long slits to allow steam to escape, then pop into the oven. Bake until the pastry is well browned, maybe 40–45 minutes.

4. Remove and cool on a rack for 10–15 minutes. Place the serving plate over the pastry top and flip over. Be careful of spilling hot caramel during the flip as sometimes the tarte is quite juicy, depending on the apple you use. Make everyone admire your artistry.

5. Serve warm with whipped cream or ice cream.

# Lorenzo's Spinach Ricotta Ravioli

She was an American girl who fell in love with Italy. He was an Italian boy who fell in love with her. Mario and Lise began their life together in Tuscany, homesteading on a farm without running water or electricity. They were nearly self-sufficient, living off the land and making everything from olive oil to Vin Santo. Soon, they made Lorenzo.

Lise wanted Lorenzo to experience America, and that is how Lorenzo found himself at the Greenwood School for 7th and 8th grades, where he and Woods soon became fast friends. After graduation he returned to Italy for high school. Those years passed quickly, and we were shocked when we heard the news. Lorenzo, having come to California for college, had been diagnosed with Leukemia during his first week of school. This was the beginning of what would become an epic journey for their entire family. After a year of treatment, Lorenzo's cancer returned, and he required a bone marrow transplant. He would need a place to recover before he could go back to Italy. That is how we had the good fortune of sharing a year of healing with Lise, Mario, and Lorenzo at our home on the mountain. We would tell many stories over dinner, usually on the themes of food and farms. One afternoon, Lise and Mario taught us how to make Lorenzo's favorite: spinach raviolis. Making pasta is most fun when there are many hands to help. This is the best ravioli we have ever tasted.

MAKES 6 GENEROUS SERVINGS

FILLING

fresh spinach (one large plastic bag full,
    about 1 pound, no stems)

1 pound fresh cow's milk ricotta cheese
½ cup Parmesan cheese
1 teaspoon nutmeg
½ teaspoon salt

1. Wash spinach and cook thoroughly in a covered pot without added water on low heat.

2. Drain the spinach, making sure to really get out all of the water. Form it into three balls, each one a bit smaller than a tennis ball (makes for easier handling when cutting). Cut the spinach up as finely as possible.

3. In a medium sized bowl, mix together spinach, ricotta, Parmesan, nutmeg, and salt. Then taste. It should be flavorful. Set aside.

PASTA
1 pound flour
⅓ pound semolina
2 teaspoons salt
5 eggs

1. Mix dry ingredients in a large bowl.

2. Next, make a well in the flour and break all of the eggs into the well. Mix using your fingers. Transfer mixture to a large cutting board for kneading.

3. "Knead the flour on a cutting board (using more flour to avoid any sticking) until it is the texture of a baby's bottom," says Lise. After kneading, roll the ball in flour and put the dough in a plastic bag to rest for half an hour.

4. Clean the cutting board, sprinkle fresh flour on the board, and roll the dough out. Slice it with a sharp knife into 2-inch strips. Roll it through the pasta maker on the #1 setting twice and then once on each successive setting through setting #6. Don't stop once you

have started rolling! Lay out the thin sheets of fresh pasta on a big cloth the size of a pillowcase, without overlapping.

5. Put spoonfuls of spinach ricotta filling every 2 inches along one side of a long pasta strip, and then fold over on itself. Seal all the edges before cutting. Cut into classic ravioli squares with a crimping wheel.

6. When finished, lay the raviolis on a heavy cloth, without touching, to dry slightly. This will use half of the pasta dough, and the extra can be refrigerated for up to three days. These can also be made and frozen.

7. Boil ravioli gently in a large covered pot with salted water for less than 5 minutes, while you prepare the sauce.

SAUCE
1 stick unsalted butter
1 cup sage leaves
$\frac{1}{2}$ teaspoon salt

1. Heat frying pan and add butter and salt. Let sage slowly brown in melted butter over a low heat.

2. Remove cooked ravioli with a slotted spoon and place into frying pan with butter and sage. Cook them a bit in the pan. (Not too much! You don't want to overcook the filling.)

3. Spoon onto warm plates and serve with freshly grated Parmesan cheese.

Buon Appetito!

# Coco's Chocolate Cake

Nobody loved chocolate more than your grandfather Coco. It's how he got his name. As a little boy, Coco (then known as Coleman) went to visit his two uncles in Salisbury, Connecticut, the town where his mother grew up. During his stay, they went on an arduous hike to the top of neighboring Mount Raga. It was a cold and rainy day for a hike, but Coleman bravely kept up with his two uncles. Having arrived at the summit, they opened a thermos of steaming hot chocolate. This was the first time Coleman had ever tasted such a beverage. He went absolutely wild over it, to the great delight of his uncles. In that moment, they decided to give him the nickname of "Hot Chocolate." But by the time they returned home, it had been shortened to "Coco." Coco considered the best part of any meal to be dessert, as long as there was chocolate involved. This particular recipe often caused him to levitate from his chair in sheer bliss.

MAKES ONE 8-INCH
DOUBLE-LAYER CAKE

unsalted butter, softened, for pans
¾ cup unsweetened cocoa powder, plus more for pans
1½ cups all-purpose flour
1½ cups sugar
1½ teaspoons baking soda
¾ teaspoon baking powder
¾ teaspoon salt
2 large eggs
¾ cup low-fat buttermilk

¾ cup warm water

3 tablespoons safflower oil

1 teaspoon pure vanilla extract

1. Pre-heat oven to 350 degrees. Butter two 8-inch round cake pans (2 inches deep); dust with cocoa. Sift cocoa, flour, sugar, baking soda, baking powder, and salt into the bowl of a mixer. Beat on low speed until just combined. Raise speed to medium, and add eggs, buttermilk, water, oil, and vanilla. Beat until smooth, about 3 minutes.

2. Divide batter between pans. Bake until set and a toothpick inserted into the centers comes out clean, about 35 minutes. Let cool for 15 minutes. Turn out from pans. Transfer, face-up, to wire racks. Let cool completely.

CHOCOLATE FROSTING (MAKES FOUR CUPS)

2¼ cups confectioners' sugar

¼ cup unsweetened cocoa powder

pinch of salt

6 ounces cream cheese, room temperature

1½ sticks unsalted butter, softened

9 ounces bittersweet chocolate, melted (a double boiler is helpful) and cooled slightly

¾ cup creme fraiche or sour cream

1. Sift together sugar, cocoa, and salt.

2. In a separate bowl, beat cream cheese and butter with a mixer on medium-high speed until smooth. Reduce speed to medium-low; gradually add sugar-cocoa mixture, and beat until combined. Pour in chocolate in a slow, steady stream. Add creme fraiche; beat until combined. Frosting can be refrigerated for up to five days. Bring to room temperature and beat before using.

3. Spread 2 cups of chocolate frosting onto top of one cooled layer. Top with remaining layer; frost top and sides with remaining 2 cups of frosting.

Can be refrigerated overnight.

# Winter Luxury Pumpkin Pie

I f you don't have a Winter Luxury pumpkin, don't panic! You can substitute any combination of pumpkin, butternut squash, and garnet yams. My favorite alternative is a blend of half garnet yam and half butternut squash.

MAKES 2 REGULAR PIES
OR 1 BIG ONE

1. Pre-heat oven to 350 degrees. Take a medium-sized Winter Luxury pumpkin (around 8-inches in diameter) and quarter it. Remove the seeds and place pumpkin slices skin down in a large roasting pan that has ½-inch of water covering the bottom.

2. Cover lightly with foil and bake for 1 hour or until pumpkin meat is easily pierced with a knife. Remove from oven and let cool. Scrape the cooked pumpkin into a bowl and set aside; there should be at least 5 cups.

3. While the pumpkin is roasting, make the crust.

CRUST INGREDIENTS

2 packages of graham crackers (There are usually 9 whole crackers per package.)

20 really good ginger snaps (approximately 2-inch diameter in size)

2 sticks unsalted butter, melted over low heat

4 tablespoons sugar

½ teaspoon sea salt

1. Put both packages of the graham crackers into your food processor and blend thoroughly. If you don't have a food processor, you can put them in a plastic bag and crush finely with a rolling pin. Transfer to a bowl large enough for all the crust ingredients.

2. Repeat process with the ginger snaps, adding them to the bowl along with the sugar and salt.

3. After mixing these dry ingredients, stir in the melted butter and blend well.

4. Pour almost half of the cookie crust mixture into each pie dish (if using two), patting it to make a fairly thick crust (about ½-inch thick). You will want to put some aside to sprinkle on top of the pies when they cool.

FILLING

5 cups of roasted pumpkin

2½ cups of half and half

4 eggs

2 teaspoons fresh ginger, finely chopped (Cut the skin off the root, slice, and then chop in the processor or by hand.)

2 teaspoons nutmeg

2 teaspoons cinnamon

2 teaspoons cardamom

1½ teaspoons sea salt

½ teaspoon ground cloves

2 teaspoons vanilla

1 cup brown sugar

½ cup white sugar

1. Transfer roasted pumpkin into a food processor. Blend with the half and half until smooth.

2. In another bowl, whisk the eggs and add in the ginger, nutmeg, cinnamon, cardamom, salt, cloves, vanilla, and both sugars.

3. Combine the pumpkin and the egg mixture, stirring well.

4. Pour into pie pans and bake, turning the pies every 20 minutes so that the crust browns evenly. It will take approximately 45 minutes to an hour for the filling to set. When ready, take out and place on a rack to cool.

5. Sprinkle with the extra cookie crust mixture that you set aside earlier. Enjoy just as is or with whipped cream.

Best to refrigerate any that is left over.

# Peter's Weekend Waffles

eter's waffles are legendary. The gently intoxicating smell of cinnamon and apples has become the traditional wake-up call for weekend breakfasts at our home in Fern Canyon. Wafting through the house, their aroma can lure even the sleepiest guests out of their roosts. Easily accommodating four to forty, Peter encourages everybody at the table to have their fill of the crunchy yet fluffy delicacies. Served with fresh berries, warm syrup, and butter, many say that Peter's waffles are one of his greatest accomplishments. Here is the recipe in Peter's own words:

MAKES 6 LARGE WAFFLES
(BETTER MAKE ENOUGH
FOR SECONDS!)

"To Bisquick or not, that is the question."

If yes, then 2 cups Bisquick (plus additional ingredients)

If no, then the from scratch ingredients are:
1¾ cups all-purpose flour
2 teaspoons baking powder
½ teaspoon salt
1 tablespoon granulated sugar
(plus additional ingredients)

5–6 eggs
½ cup unsalted butter
1¾ cups whole milk
1 grated apple
cinnamon and nutmeg
½ teaspoon pure vanilla extract (optional)

1. Eggs: Separate and beat the egg whites into a soft meringue. Set aside.

2. Butter: Melt ½ cup (1 stick) unsalted butter, not oil. Set aside.

3. Dry Ingredients: In large mixing bowl, combine all of these plus cinnamon (lots), nutmeg, 1 grated apple, butter, milk, and vanilla extract. Then mix.

4. Fold in the egg whites . . . and then make a latte while you wait for your customers. Don't forget to gently warm the maple syrup, put out the butter, and if the spirit moves you, slice strawberries adding some lemon juice and a dash of sugar.

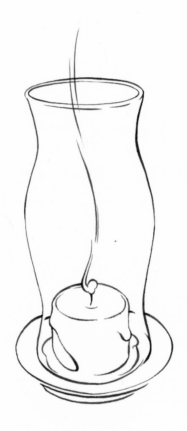

# A Bow of Gratitude

*"In the end, these things matter most:*
*How well did you love?*
*How fully did you live?*
*How deeply did you let go?"*
– BUDDHA

Writing this letter to the three of you has been a journey, complete with life lessons and unexpected blessings—not unlike becoming a parent. In fact, this book began, like you, as only a sparkle in my mind's eye, a feeling of something that needed to be. The possibility became ignited in the presence of family and friends, whose gentle listening, encouragement, and support gave me the courage to begin. Like all good midwives, they calmed me through the labor of envisioning, guided me through my fears of not knowing, and handed my bundle of ideas back with total assurance, confident that I would know how to proceed. To Nina Simons, Patricia Zeigler, Anna Muirhead Hawken McKay, Sherry Stein, Jonathan Browning, Kristine Tompkins, Paula Reynolds, and Kaye Jones; thank you for believing. Unending love and gratitude to Peter; you are truly my Ganesh.

Like a newborn, the project felt fragile yet full of potential. Its needs required round-the-clock attention, often keeping me awake at night with its whimpers. Writing became rewriting, considerations needed reconsidering, a seemingly strong concept might look simply anemic the next day. I was still wearing my bathrobe at noon, trying to get the right words to tell the story. Doubts would appear, uninvited. On Thursday mornings I would stumble into my weekly meeting with Devika Brandt, clutching my ideas in a smudged binder that overflowed with sticky notes and paperclips. Devika has all the qualities of a fairy godmother, poet, English teacher, and therapist. The same way that she taught each of you to write from your heart, she coaxed the story along, clarifying the voice, encouraging it to reveal something more. She helped me to reframe doubt into curiosity, created a safe space for exploration of ideas, and fiercely edited each successive draft, evicting unnecessary commas and suggesting elegant revisions for awkward sentences. Thank you, Devika, for accompanying me every step of the way.

They say that if your muse is late for work, start without her. It just so happened that during this time I found a muse who could be reached both by phone and internet, and she even had a comfy office where we could meet each month. Vanda Marlow is a living muse. She taught me to recognize, welcome, and celebrate a muse of my own. Scattering inspiration over my efforts like glitter, Vanda's bright presence offered a consistent beacon, guiding me back to port even in the darkest of moments. Thank you, Vanda, for your humor, intelligence, poetry, and great tips on where to shop.

A year and a half passed, and by then the book had moved from infancy into toddlerhood, wobbling around with a new momentum, seeking balance and dreaming of grace. Unfortunately, as babies go, it was not very attractive. My lack of computer savvy left me with a manuscript that was a stammering pile of pages in oversized font, devoid of any consistent structure. That was when Richard Whittaker offered to help. He arrived early on a Sunday morning and dedicated hours to the cleaning up of the manuscript, his only compensation being one of Peter's waffles. Squeezed into my closet of an office (along with the cat, the bird, and myself), he deftly tapped instructions into the keys, transforming my efforts into a professional-looking first draft. And he didn't stop there. He then gave it a thorough read-through, offering suggestions that strengthened the stories and my enthusiasm. It isn't easy to ask others for help. I was hesitant to request too much for fear of imposing. Richard's consistent generosity provided a new experience of friendship, beyond the calculations of giving and receiving. Thank you, Richard, for making it so easy to ask and for revealing the gift of supportive community.

As the project matured, it began to ask questions. Where does meaning reside? Do the stories touch that place? Are they worthy of the effort? These questions reverberated within. Sticking with what I knew to be true in my bones was the best I could do. Not unlike that night many years ago when, discarding the professional advice in the baby books, we discovered the joy of intuitive parenting, a sense of freedom entered into my spirit and the project. I learned to trust this creative process, which continued to reveal an inherent quality of synchronicity. Satisfying solutions to my various questions would emerge with the simple passing of time. During this period, I also asked dear friends and family for their help. Generously taking the time to offer feedback and suggestions, their support carried me across the finish line. Deep gratitude to Jane Morton, Peggie Buckley, Hilary Hood, Zenobia Barlow, Mel Zeigler, Tim Dye, Marci Ellison, Nancy Biffar, Katie Clark, Kenny Ausubel, Quincy Imhoff, Carla Crane, Lise Apetoff, Sally Ward, Marsha Angus, Pat Zylius, Corrine Oishi, Amy Tobin, Patricia, Anna, Sherry, Nina, Kaye, Paula, Peter, Charlie, Ana, Lindley, Janie, Michael, Diana, and the three of you for honest feedback and timely kindnesses. A big *Danke schön* to Cheri de Haas and Rolf Knitter for their long distance help with the German text. Ayelet Maida's meticulous guidance through the process of making a book combined with Aya Morton's artistic vision and stunning execution of the illustrations depicting the images of our home have instilled this letter with an appealing, well-organized beauty. Thank you to one and all.

The wisdom gained from family and friends has been a fundamental underpinning for both this book and our daily lives. I would like to thank Marc Barasch, Frank Osteseski, Jane Bryan-Jones, and Eliza Martin-Jatsek for their guidance and insights, founded on the understanding that life is precious and living fully into it is our best response. Your poetry, writing, and teachings bring meaning and comfort to each day. And of course, a bow of gratitude to Buddha and the Dharma.

Throughout your childhood, Peter and I shared the task of parenting with several individuals who deserve acknowledgement and loving appreciation for their dedication to our family. Great thanks to Uschi, Eva, Imke, Catherine, Ivan, Dani, Ana, and Jerusha. Our deepest bow must go to Sung Ja Cho, who for over twenty years has made a clean and welcoming home, where everyone feels nurtured. Thank you Cho for your endless loyalty and love.

In the Hindu tradition, after the Householder phase is complete, an individual then becomes a Retired Person. This third chapter is a time when, with the responsibilities of the household diminished, one is free to "involve in more active worship." I enjoy this idea, because it feels like a call to engage with everyone and everything in as meaningful a way as possible. What could be better?

Peter and I delight in seeing you taking on life as young adults. As you have grown, so have we. Just like being parents, growing up is never finished. You are our teachers and we continue to learn from you. We cherish our time together and thank you for being such loving companions on this journey. Every moment has been made brighter by your presence. You have, indeed, filled this life with light.

May you always feel at home wherever you go,

Your Loving Mom(ma)

# A Few Favorite Books

ON CHILDBIRTH

Gaskin, Ina May. *Ina May's Guide to Childbirth*. New York: Bantum Dell, March, 2003.

———. *Spiritual Midwifery*. Summertown, Tennessee: Book Publishing Company, 1975.

ON EARLY CHILDHOOD

Baldwin Dancy, Rahima. *You Are Your Child's First Teacher: What Parents Can do With and For Their Children from Birth to Age Six*. Canada: Random House/Celestial Arts, 1989.

Liedloff, Jean. *The Continuum Concept: In Search of Happiness Lost*. Cambridge: Da Capo Press, 1985.

Small, Merideth F. *Our Babies, Ourselves*. New York: Random House/Anchor Books, 1999.

ON POSITIVE DISCIPLINE

Nelson, Jane. *Positive Discipline*. New York: Ballantine Books, 1996. Also by Jane Nelson: *Positive Discipline for Preschoolers, Positive Discipline For Teenagers, Positive Discipline A–Z*

ON YOGA

Scaravelli, Vanda. *Awakening the Spine: The Stress-free New Yoga that Works with the Body to Restore Health, Vitality, and Energy*. New York: Harper Collins Publishers, 1991.

Schiffman, Erich. Yoga: *The Spirit and Practice of Moving into Stillness*. New York: Pocket Books, 1996.

White, Ganga. *Yoga Beyond Belief: Insights to Awaken and Deepen Your Practice.* Berkeley, California: North Atlantic Books, 2007.

ON KINDNESS

Boorstein, Seymour. *Who's Talking Now?* Bloomington, Indiana: AuthorHouse, 2011.

Boorstein, Sylvia. *Happiness is an Inside Job.* New York: Ballantine Books, 2008.

———. *Pay Attention For Goodness' Sakes: Practicing the Perfections of the Heart, The Buddhist Path of Kindness.* New York: Ballantine Books, 2002.

Dass, Ram. *Be Love Now, The Path of the Heart.* New York: Harper Collins Publisher, 2010.

Goldstein, Joseph. *Insight Meditation, The Practice of Freedom.* Boston: Shambala Press, 1993.

Rosenberg, Marshall B. *The Surprising Purpose of Anger: Beyond Anger Management: Finding the Gift.* California: PuddleDancer Press, 2005.

Salzberg, Sharon. *Loving Kindness: The Revolutionary Art of Happiness.* Boston: Shambhala Press, 1995.

———. *Voices of Insight.* Boston: Shambhala Press, 1999.

ON BUDDHISM

Batchelor, Stephen. *Buddhism Without Beliefs.* New York: Riverhead Books, 1997.

ON BEING A HUMAN BEING

Brooks, David. *The Social Animal.* New York: Random House, 2011.

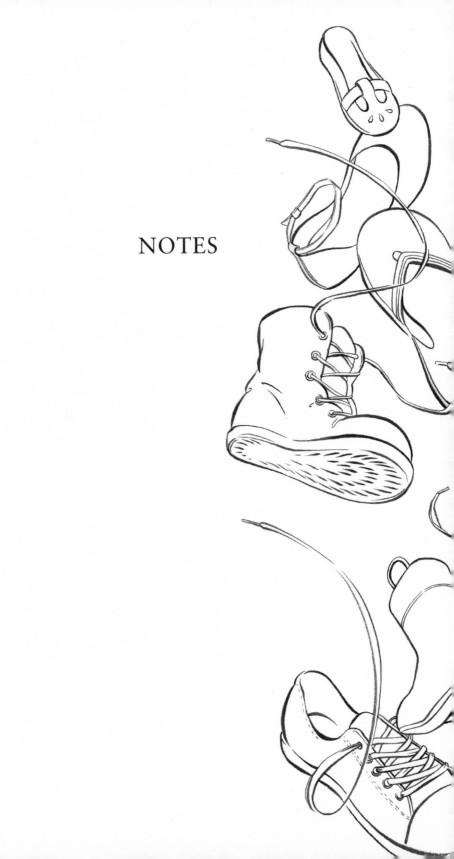

NOTES

NOTES

NOTES

NOTES

NOTES

Published by
Rabbit Rabbit Press
PMB# 276
38 Miller Avenue
Mill Valley, California 94941

Limited edition prints and other artwork from *The Road Home* are available online through Rabbit Rabbit Press. www.rabbitrabbitpress.com, info@rabbitrabbitpress.com

Illustrations © Aya Morton. www.ayamorton.com, aya@rabbitrabbitpress.com
Book design and production by Ayelet Maida, A/M Studios

Rabbit Rabbit Press is committed to preserving ancient forests and natural resources. By printing this title on 30% postconsumer recycled paper, processed chlorine-free, we have saved: 2 trees (40' tall and 6-8" diameter), 1 million BTUs of total energy, 125 pounds of greenhouse gases, 678 gallons of wastewater, and 45 pounds of solid waste. Environmental impact estimates were made using the Environmental Defense Paper Calculator. www.edf.org/papercalculator

Our printer, Thomson-Shore, Inc., is a member of Green Press Initiative, a nonprofit program dedicated to supporting authors, publishers, and suppliers in their efforts to reduce their use of fiber obtained from endangered forests.
www.greenpressinitiative.org

Printed in the United States of America.

2  3  4  5  6  7  8  9  10  TS  17  16  15  14  13